Step-by-Step
College Admissions Counseling

A Guide for High School Students and Parents

2020 Fifth Edition

Table of Contents

PART I JUNIOR YEAR

Use the Step by Step College Counseling Approach

1. To stay organized through the process.

2. To keep the process as simple as possible

3. To move forward one manageable step at a time

4. Because it is proven to help students plan for, become accepted to, and to graduate on time from a best fit college

5. Because it was designed with you in mind and, simply put, it works!

<u>Is College Right for Me?</u>

Why go to College?

Did you know that a college education is likely to help:

1. significantly increase your financial income over a lifetime

2. contribute to your life experiences, passions and interests

3. you learn about specific careers

4. allow you to sample many different courses and areas of study

5. create an environment for developing lasting relationships with peers, faculty and administrators

6. provide opportunities to participate in new and refine existing sports, clubs, hobbies and artistic talents

7. allow you to create lifelong habits of good health and mental fortitude

8. find opportunities to travel the world.

9. create opportunities where you can learn about the world and your place in it.

Are there other reasons someone might attend college?

One common reason people choose to attend college:

The statistics! (Consider the below national averages for earnings per level of education)

Doctoral Degree	$89,400
Master's Degree	$62,300
Bachelor's Degree	$52,200
Associate's Degree	$38,200
Some College	$36,800
High School Graduate	$30,400
Some High School	$23,400

(Source: US Government BLS)

The best reason to attend college:

To learn about yourself, the world, and potential career options

Few high school students have sufficient life experiences to know what they want to do with their lives, or are able to shape their career goals.

College, being very different from high school, provides an exposure to many professors who share their subjects in a more practical manner. They may teach you subject content yet may also explain how their material relates to the many interesting occupations in the world of work.

College is a great place to meet people like you and some not so like you. It provides opportunities to learn about new things, ideas, activities, places and, potentially, much more.

It is fine to be **considering** your major at this point in your life! Many students find that with time and work, college can help them shape their ideas about what success is and how to get there.

Copyright 2020

How will you contribute to your college environment?

Many college graduates say that learning from their peers when in college is as gratifying as is learning from their coursework. Researchers state that better than half of what is learned in college is learned outside the classroom.

Also, most college admission officers (through your application) want to know what you will contribute to their campuses. Therefore, it is important to think about what role you will play in contributing to your future classmates' college experiences.

What and how will you contribute to your college environment? Be honest and generous with yourself.

To start, consider the ways that you add to your peer groups, classes, and high school overall. Many of those traits will inevitably be repeated in the college environment.

Some examples are: I bring humor to my peer group. I am outgoing and friendly. I am a contributor to points in history or English classes. I am persuasive. I am an athlete and a musician. I am creative or stylish. So on…

Consider how you could imagine yourself positively influencing the following college environments with your own skills and personality. Here are some places/ways where that can happen:

1. Your classes

2. The residence hall/ dorm room

3. Making positive change/ Leadership on campus

4. On the athletic field/ on stage/ in the art studio

5. Socially with peers and friends

6. Spiritual life

7. Community service/ volunteer opportunities

8. Other

Assignment: Write a short one paragraph essay titled, "What will I contribute to my college campus?". Tell how you see yourself contributing to your college environment in at least two ways.

Standardized Tests in College Admissions Test Preparation and Test Timing

The three most important factors in college admissions remain:

1) Grades/GPA (Grade Point Average)
2) Level of course difficulty: Often identified when looking at a student's grade point average (honors/AP)
3) Standardized tests:
ACT Test
SAT Reasoning Test
SAT Subject Tests

(Given the importance of #3, testing is worth further comment.)

ACT, SAT, and SAT Subject Tests

Admissions tests are seen, by most colleges, as standardized ways to measure how likely students will be at succeeding during his/her first year of college.
Keep in mind: generally, the higher the scores a school reports, the more challenging a school will be to attend.

Which test is right for you?

You may have taken the Pre-ACT and/or the PSAT test and they can be used as a proxies for the ACT and SAT. The proxy test providing the highest result, is the test for which you must prepare. Most colleges require standardized tests for admissions. **Unless your past standardized testing scores have been at least in the 90 percentile: PREP!** It is important to be prepared to take the SAT or the ACT. Either a prep book, a prep class or private tutor is necessary before sitting for the first time to take either test. Thirty hours of prep is recommended. If you have no pre-test to gauge which test is 'your best', see more information in this section detailing the difference between the two tests.

All colleges accept the SAT or ACT equally, so put effort into the one that is best for you!

ACT / SAT Comparison:

Since all colleges accept both the SAT Reasoning test (with essay) and the ACT test (with writing) there are various ways to determine which test is right for you.

Consider the below chart depicting the differences between each of the tests:

	ACT	SAT
Dates	Sept, Oct, Dec, Feb, April, June	Oct, Nov, Dec, Jan, March, May, June, Aug
Test Structure and Format	ACT	New SAT
Length	3 hours, 35 min (with optional Writing Test)	3 hours, 50 minutes (with optional Essay)
Structure	4 sections (English, Math, Reading, Science) plus an Optional Essay	4 sections (Evidence-Based Reading, Writing, Math without a calculator, Math with a calculator) plus an Optional Essay
Scoring	ACT	New SAT
	Composite of 1-36 based on average scores from the 4 test sections	Score is out of 1600: 800 for Math, 800 for Evidence-Based Reading and Writing
	4 scores of 1-36 for each test	Optional Essay receives a separate score
Score	Optional Writing Test score of 1-36 (not included in the overall)	Subscores and insight scores available
Guessing Penalty	No penalty for wrong answers	No penalty for wrong answers
Sending Score History	You decide which score is sent	Not yet known
Content	ACT	New SAT
		Reading Comprehension
		Words in Context
Reading	Reading Comprehension	Evidence Based
	Arithmetic	Algebra
	Algebra	Data Analysis
	Geometry	Geometry
	Algebra II	Trigonometry
Math	Trigonometry	Algebra II
	Analysis	Science Insight Score
	Interpretation	
	Evaluation	Provided
	Basic Content	
Science	Problem Solving	
	The Essay: Writing Test	
Writing and language	English Test: Writing & Language multiple-choice questions	Optional final section 50 minutes Separate score Tests Reading, Analysis, and Writing Skills
	Optional final section	
	40 minutes	
	Not included in composite score	Topic comes from a 750-word passage to be read on Test Day
	Topic presents conversations around contemporary issues	

Tests grammatical and rhetorical skills

Summary Differences between the SAT and ACT

1. The SAT has a greater focus on History & Social Studies passages, while the ACT requires more Science reading.

2. Both focus on Algebra, but the SAT has a greater emphasis on Data Analysis & Problem Solving.

3. Both essays are optional, but the SAT essay requires additional text analysis.

4. The SAT has a 'No Calculator' Math section.

5. The SAT Math section has 'grid-in' questions and Item Sets.

6. To an extent, ACT math is not as difficult as SAT math.

Test Registration and Sending Scores

How to Register/ Send SAT Reasoning and Subject Tests/ Scores

Go to www.collegeboard.com
To register for the SAT you must create a free account on their website.
If you already registered for an SAT online, you must use your same user name when you have scores sent to colleges.
You have up to a week after the test to have four free score reports sent to colleges. If this is your first test, there is no need to send scores to colleges now. If in doubt, ask your counselor. Scores will be available online about 3 weeks after a test has been taken.
If you go online to have scores sent using regular delivery to colleges, scores are sent 3-5 weeks after the request is made. If you rush the reports, the scores are sent 2 business days after the request is made.

SAT Score Cancellations

In very unusual or extreme cases, scores of the Reasoning Test or Subject Tests (taken the same day) can be canceled. This may be appropriate if you became very ill during the test administration or if you miss a complete section. Cancellation is not recommended simply because you did not perform well. Contact your counselor if there is any doubt, immediately after the test day when we have time to discuss it. Cancellations can occur on the test day or up through the Wednesday after the test. For same day cancellations, ask the test proctor for a cancellation form fill it out and hand it in before you leave.

Canceling Scores after You Leave the Test Center

You may decide to cancel your scores after you leave the test center. We must receive your request to cancel scores in writing by **11:59 p.m. Eastern Time, on the Wednesday after the test date**. You cannot submit cancellation requests by phone or email—your signature is required.

Provide the following information:
Your name, address, sex, birth date, and registration number
Test date
Test center number

Name of test you are canceling—either SAT Reasoning Test or Subject Test (please remember you cannot cancel scores for only one Subject Test

Where to Send the Cancellation Request

Please label your request **"Attention: SAT Score Cancellation"** and send it by one of the following methods:
Fax: (610) 290-8978
Overnight delivery via U.S. Postal Service Express Mail (U.S. only):
SAT Score Cancellation P.O. Box 6228, Princeton, NJ 08541-6228

Other overnight mail service or courier (U.S. or international):
SAT Score Cancellation 225 Phillips Boulevard, Ewing, NJ 08618USA

How to Register for/ send my ACT scores?

Go to www.act.org

Create an account and register for the test date you prefer

Reports can be sent at no charge to a few colleges if the colleges are identified at the time of registration. Subsequent score reports are sent for a fee.

ACT registration questions? Live customer service is available Monday through Friday, 8:00 a.m.-8:00 p.m., Central Time at (319) 337-1270.

How to Cancel ACT sent requests or to delete ACT scores

If you requested that a particular college receive a score report, but decide after taking the test that you'd rather not have the school see your results, you can request that the score report *not be* sent—but you have to do it quickly. As per the ACT, "The deadline for adding, changing, or canceling college and high school reports is the Thursday noon (central time) immediately after the regularly scheduled Saturday test date." However, keep this in mind: You will not be able to see your scores before you cancel sending them, and the score is still a part of your ACT score record. Canceling the score reports doesn't delete the score from your record. If, after you get your scores, you decide that you do want to send them to schools, you can have score reports sent.

If you would like to delete a score permanently, so that it is no longer a part of your record at all, that is also an option. The ACT website says that in order to have the results from an administration removed from your record you need to send them a request in writing. Once they receive your request, the ACT will send you a form to complete and send back, after which they will permanently remove your record for that test date from their files, and all scores from that test date will be deleted.

More Testing Information

Subject Tests

Some 100 colleges either recommend or require the College Board subject tests. No more than three are called for. Subject tests are a way for students to show a particularly strong ability in a given subject. If required or recommended, any three can be selected except in certain cases. Some health, engineering or architecture programs may require a certain math or science subject test.

Normally, the subject tests are geared toward high school junior year level ability. Because these tests are subject specific, some may need to be taken in freshman or sophomore years. For example the strong chemistry student who completed the course in sophomore year will take the subject test in sophomore year.

Students planning to take the tests must speak with the subject teacher in high school to gain a sense of preparedness based on the high school curriculum. Usually, additional prep for the test is necessary. Like SAT/ACT tests, preparation is highly recommended. Speak with your counselor about these.

Lastly, because subject tests are subject specific, June is generally the best month to take them because prep occurs in high school for final exams in subjects that may be the same as the anticipated Subject Tests.

Colleges use subject tests for admissions and for placement, once the student attends college.

Advanced Placement (AP) Testing Information

These are courses and tests meant to expose students to college level work. Some high schools require students to take the AP exam if a student is taking the course; others make the AP exam optional and may have a separate final exam for the course. Students should always take the AP exam if the course is taken because the score reports are separate from SAT and Subject tests score reports. Therefore, poor performances do not have to be reported. Further, all AP score reports are not sent to colleges until July after senior year, well after students are admitted. Students will self-report AP scores on the college applications, where asked.

Students are encouraged to consider AP exams like subject tests. If they are strong in a particular subject, even without taking the AP course, they might still take the exam. Again, not all AP test scores need be reported to colleges.

AP courses and tests (with a 3 or better score at most colleges, 4 or better at top colleges), will not only give the benefit of lightening your course load in college as these scores on AP tests count for credit, but also, often course registration is opened to students based on credits achieved, so you may be in the front of the class when it comes to course selection throughout your time in college as a result of acceptable AP scores.

Resume Writing

Why create a resume?

To highlight your high school academic and extra-curricular experiences in a succinct, organized and easy to read fashion
To hand to admissions officers and coaches on school visits and interviews
To learn the skills necessary to apply for jobs throughout life
To make a professional impression

General Guidelines for Writing a Resume

Avoid all abbreviations

Keep to one page

Make sure it is easy to read, following a consistent format

Personal style may be reflected, but try not to deviate much from templates found online.

No colored ink

Includes information from grades 9-12 only

Resume sections should be presented in reverse chronology, which means list your most recent activities first.

The first section after the heading is the most important to the reader (for ALL students academics comes first, -for adult resumes, employment comes first.)

Resume Sections

1. Contact information (the heading)
2. Academic

(The following student activity sections should be listed in order of importance/significance/time to the student.)
3. Extracurricular
4. Employment (aim to include dates, job titles, companies, work responsibilities and successful outcomes)
5. Volunteer Activities and Responsibilities
6. Hobbies and Interests

Resume Writing Check List

Check each to be sure you have followed the basic rules for writing an effective resume.

For all activities, if space allows, include: what you got out of the activity, what skills you used, and what you accomplished, not what you did, as that is usually self-explanatory.

The resume is only one page

Use a professional email address

If possible, print resume on quality paper (white or cream)

Be consistent in style and format (for example, font, bold face, use of bullets and or dates)

Avoid using personal pronouns such as I, me, or my

Make sure your font size is at least 10 point

Be honest. Do not exaggerate or falsify information

Avoid the use of acronyms and abbreviations

Create your resume with activities starting the summer before grade 9

Keep your resume updated and current

To keep it easy to find, include the date and time in the title of the document saved

Email or upload to locations online for easy access from anywhere

John C. Cardinal

37 Wildwood Street, Garden City, Maryland 21201

Home phone: (410) 756 1234, Mobile Phone: (410) 738 1234,

jcardinal@gmail.com

Academic Highlights

High School, Class of 2019, Any town, Any State,

GPA: 3.75, Honor Roll for six quarters as of junior year. 3 AP courses and 2 honors courses, thus far

Scores: AP U.S. History: 3, and AP Biology: 5

SAT Reasoning:	Math: 630, Reading: 660 Writing: 590, March 2015
SAT Subject Tests:	Math II: 730, Chemistry: 700 U.S. History: 720, June 2015

Courses Taken (by end of senior year)

4 years of math	3 years of French
4 years of history	4 years of English
4 years of theology	3 years of sciences

Athletic Highlights Eastern Independent League, Division 2

Lacrosse: Coach Craig Whaler. Position: Close Defense

Varsity: grades 9-12. Senior year: Team captain. I was a starter sophomore year. Attended both: Cardigan Mountain Lacrosse Camp junior year and New England Top 150, senior year Supported our team last season to a 5-4 record.

Wrestling: Coach Tim Chickenwinger. Starting 14: grades 9-12.

New England Qualifier during junior year, at 189 lb weight class, ranked 9th in New England with a record of 17-8. This year: will be in 215 lb weight class.

Golf: Coach John Foshizzle. In top-6 for both junior and senior years Handicap: 20

Extra-Curricular Activities/Jobs/ Hobbies/ Volunteering

Avid skier and snowboarder, Ski instructor at Loon Mountain, S.C.U.B.A. certified, American Archer, and rifle sharpshooter; Youth Group Leader at my church, Math Club: grade 9 and 10, Peer Tutor: grade 11 and 12. Employed: junior summer at Meadow Breeze Day Camp.

NOTES

College Admissions Terms and Concepts

Education Types

Primary School (pre-kindergarten through 8th grade)
Secondary School Diploma (grades 9-12)
Technical Certificate
Undergraduate Degrees:
Associate Degree 2-year
Bachelor Degree 4-year (BS, BA, BFA)
Advanced degrees:
Master's Degree   1-to-3 years (MBA, M. Ed., MSW)
Terminal Degree 4-plus years (PhD, LLM, MD)

College Types

1. Pre-professional (also known as Liberal Arts. Graduate school is intended.)

Art, History, Psychology, English, Pre-medicine, Pre-veterinarian,
Pre-law.

2. Professional (Graduate school is not required.)

Nursing, Accounting, etc.

Core Curriculum

A college's Core Curriculum, also known as a college's Distribution
Requirement (or General Education Requirement) are required courses all
students must complete before graduation, regardless of major choice.

Creating a College List

A well thought out list often numbers between six and ten colleges, but can be more.

Likely, Target and Reach Colleges

Likely colleges are generally those less rigorous for you given your academic profile. Your SAT/ACT scores are typically 50 points higher than the mid-range score reported on collegeboard.com.
Keep in mind that Likely colleges should be appealing due to academic and or extracurricular reasons. Many Likely colleges will offer generous merit-based aid dollars.
Admission to Likely colleges is reasonably assured.

Target colleges are those where student test scores fall within the range of those accepted, and reported on collegeboard.com (within whose average SAT/ACT scores match the students' scores).
A student can call these colleges target. This classification should include the bulk of the colleges on your list.
Admission to these colleges is probable.

Reach colleges are schools for which a student's scores are below the midrange. These are often the "dream" schools and similarly those that provide you with the lowest percentage chance of gaining entrance. Keep in mind that Very Selective and Most Selective schools are typically considered to be Reaches for all students. Admission to these colleges is unlikely.

Typically, selective colleges admit less than 50% of all applicants and very selective colleges typically admit less than 30% of all applicants.

Keep in mind

Substantial test prep and or continued academic work can add to your scores. Consider this when classifying colleges as Likely, Target or Reach.

Other factors

Other factors that can affect the above college classifications can be a student's proximity to a college and a student's unique attributes. The further away from a campus a student lives, the more appealing that student is to the college. Other factors, from a college's point of view, that may make a student more desirable include musical and or athletic abilities, unique passions and interests, ethnicities, legacies, donor status and or unique ability. Gender can also play a large role; most applicants today are female and colleges strive for 50/50.

Consider average GPA's (grade point average) on various websites as broad indicators, and not as effective as standardized test scores when assessing classifications (Likely, Target, Reach).

Important College Parameters

Be aware of your preferences in each of these areas so that you are able to create lists that are appropriate to *your* needs and interests.
Selectivity
Location (urban/suburban/rural/ N, S, E, W/ international)
Size (large, medium, small)
Major (can be Undecided)
Sports (Divisional, inter- and intramural)
Activities and Special Programs
Religious/Non-religious
Greek life (fraternities/sororities)
Private or Public
Cost (including percentage of family need met, average debt at graduation)
Diversity

Four steps to researching colleges

Step One using collegeboard.org college search feature:

Assemble a large list of colleges (30+) that generally meet your interests and abilities.
How?
Complete a college search on collegeboard.org, from the home page look for College Search
Click Selectivity of school to start and progress through the search engine.
If too many colleges result from this search, go back and insert more filters (e.g.location, activities)
Stay organized. Keep your list accessible, maybe save online at the collegeboard.org.
Ask your college counselor to look over your list to reveal obvious mismatches.

Step Two using collegeboard.org website:

Filter your large list (down to as many as 10-20)
How?
One by one insert your college names into the College Quick Finder white box on www.collegeboard.org, then select the college name on the next page.
You are now at the "At a Glance" page of the college's profile on collegeboard.
For each college, consider the following data from the profile

A. Information to consider, when at the collegeboard.org "At a Glance" page:

Location
Including a map

Number of undergraduates (under Campus Life)
LESS than 4,000 students is ideal for most

Net Price Calculator is sometimes here
To estimate the true cost

B. Majors and Learning Environment

Click the All Majors tab, if you know your major, seek colleges with multiple, related majors so if you change majors, you may not need to transfer.

C. Campus Life

Number of undergraduates: Less that 4000 is better for most students.

Click tabs Activities and Sports to see what is offered.

See: pie chart on diversity: more is better!

pie chart on gender mix: often you will see more females, a plus for admissions for males

pie chart on in state and out of state mix: If you are out of state for a state school, slim slice of pie for out of state students may mean higher admission requirements, also do many go home on weekends?

D. Applying

See grey box for admit rate:

Less than 30% Very Selective

Less that 50% Selective

Click tabs for Academics and GPA and SAT and ACT scores to see how you compare:

Generally: If your scores are below the mid-range, consider it a reach school, in the mid-range, consider it a target and if your scores are above the mid-range, the college may be a safe school.

To be sure, also consider the admit rate. Although your scores may be above the mid-range, if the college is very selective, it may be a reach regardless of scores, even for the perfect 1600 SAT!

E. Paying page

Financial aid awards vary widely by college.

Sometimes the college's own Net Price calculator is here and can be started by clicking the blue button Calculate Your Net Price. If not, put Net Price Calculator in the search box on the college website.

On this page is the total cost, for both in-state and out-of-state residents

If you are applying for financial aid be sure to include affordable colleges in each of your college classifications (Reach, Target, Likely).

Rigor	Cost
3 Reach Schools	Including 1 school that is more affordable
4 Target Schools	Including 1 that is that is more affordable
3 Likely Schools	Including 1 school that is more affordable

Step Three:

Further refine your college list to a number that can be visited
How?
Go to the college website and look more critically at each college's list of clubs and organizations, and, also look at courses and majors.

When at a chosen college's website

See "Student Life" or "Current Students" to review clubs for a political and social feel of the campus.

See "Academics" section of the web site for interesting programs, honors colleges in likely colleges (for merit aid) or large universities (for a small college feel) and graduation requirements (some require internships, a thesis or comprehensive exams that may or may not fit your style and ambition).

Step Four:

Visit each of the colleges on this list.
Note: be sure to include on this list colleges from each of the previously mentioned categories (Likely, Target and Reach). Also, be sure to balance the choices given family financial considerations. After you visit, some colleges may be eliminated. Using Naviance, you will see how to find more that may be similar to the ones you like, and you may now be adding to the college list.

Staying Organized in you college planning process

It is important to stay organized during your process. Doing so will dramatically reduce senses of confusion and anxiety while equally increasing the likelihood of successfully achieving goals.

Create a system to organize all of your college related information by using folders, individually titled, for each college that you are seriously considering. In them, place flyers, catalogues and email messages. Create electronic folders in your email, one for each college, to keep track of emails to and from each college. Keep a generic email folder for colleges not on the list now. Check SPAM folders frequently!

Useful College Search Web Resources

http://www.fairtest.org List of colleges that are SAT and ACT optional

http://www.collegeboard.org Great college search engine and place for all info related to SAT Reasoning Test, SAT Subject test, AP, CSS profile (financial aid)

http://www.petersons.comVery good search tool

http://www.collegeview.com Another useful college search engine

http://www.aucc.ca/dcu For those interested in Canadian colleges and universities

http://www.hbcuconnect.com Excellent site for historically black colleges and universities

Theatre College Directory/Performing Artists

> http://collegedirectory.schooltheatre.org
>
> Bachelor of Music information
>
> http://www.peabody.jhu.edu/doubledegree

For Visual Artists

> *"AN ARTIST DRAWS A PATH TO COLLEGE"*
>
> http://chronical.com/article/an-artist-draws-a-path-to/151249/
>
> College Lists Wiki for Various Arts Majors:
>
> http://collegelists.pbworks.com
>
> National Portfolio Days
>
> http://www.portfolioday.net
>
> Slide Room
>
> http://www.slideroom.com
>
> Accepted
>
> http://www.getaccepted.com

International Colleges

www.cisabroad.com Assists American students in finding colleges in England, Ireland, Scotland, Italy, Spain, Australia and New Zealand

National Survey of Student Engagement

http://nsse.iub.edu/index.cfm NSSE is a reliable indication of the quality of education that students can receive

National Collegiate Athletic Association NCAA

http://www.ncaa.org/ Information related to NCAA, eligibility and ability to sort colleges by division and state

Campus Crime

http://ope.ed.gov/security/Search.aspGreat site for checking crime on campus

Career Related

http://www.bls.gov/oco/
Occupational Outlook Handbook- career forecasts from Uncle Sam

http://www.onetcenter.org
Great career search and info site offered by the Department of Labor

Financial Aid

http://www.fastweb.comGreat scholarship search engine, also has a college search engine

http://www.scholarshipamerica.org Another scholarship resource

http://www.scholarships.com Another scholarship search engine

http://www.finaid.com Another site for exploring private aid and scholarships

http://www.fafsa.ed.gov/ This is the government's web page for Federal Application for Free Student Aid

http://yahoo.com/education/financial_aid Good resource for other financial aid web sites

http://www.salliemae.com More information regarding student loans

http://216.74.11.178 This is a strange URL for MOLIS, which is Minority Online Information System, a web site for financial aid, among other resources

ROTC

http://www.todaysmilitary.comGain information on ROTC programs

Testing

http://www.collegeboard.org The place to register for SAT Reasoning Test and SAT Subject test, and for seeing scores and sending them to colleges

http://www.actstudent.org/ ACT test web site, for some, an alternative to the SAT

http://fairtest.org/ This site provides a list of institutions that do not require standardized tests for admissions

Students with Disabilities

http://www.finaid.org/otheraid/disabled.phtml The site for Financial Aid has a disability resources page and includes financial aid strategies and scholarship opportunities

(See also, additional information and websites later in this manual)

Disability friendly colleges

Websites at University of Arizona (a disability friendly college):
http://www.arizona.edu/
http://drc.arizona.edu/
http://www.salt.arizona.edu/

Faith-based College Sites

http://catholiccollegesonline.org Catholic campus ministries throughout the United States
http://www.campuscrusadeforchrist.orgGreat site with ability to search campuses with email addresses of current club presidents
http://www.intervarsity.org Map of US makes it easy to find campus clubs along with current president email address
http://www.navigators.org Another active Christian club with many ministries.
http://www.msanational.org/ Muslim Student Organization
http://www.hillel.org Campus organization for Jewish students

Common application for Historically Black Colleges and Universities
http://commonblackcollegeapp.com A way to apply to many HBCU's with one application

Overview

www.nacacnet.org search for a great - College Awareness and Planning

College Planning (search and search/scholarship)

www.collegedata.com

www.colleges.niche.com

www.cappex.com

www.petersons.com

www.unigo.com

www.number2.com

Financial information/planning site

www.studentaid.ed.gov

Information for first-generation college students

www.Imfirst.org

www.Raise.me

Scholarship search

www.Collegegreenlight.com

College video-tour

www.youuniversitytv.com

Learning Differences in Higher Education

Generally, learning challenges that do not require accommodations in high school do not need to be disclosed to colleges. In fact, it is illegal for a high school to disclose a learning challenge to a college in a letter of recommendation or any other way unless the student or his or her parents or guardians grant permission.

Sometimes a student with a learning challenge has learned to perform so well in high school by employing strategies and skills that no accommodations are needed in college. It is; however, sometimes wise to disclose the learning challenge to colleges as a way of describing how a student overcame adversity - a quality that shows evidence of strong personal development. This is a judgment call on the part of the student and parents with input from your counselor.

Regardless of whether accommodations are needed or not in college, students are advised to follow the college discernment process in the same way as those not seeking accommodations. Usually it is only in severe cases of learning challenges that accommodations cannot be provided by colleges.

Learning challenges needing accommodation in college by the student should be disclosed to the college (preferably) or the parent/guardian near the time of applying. Again, severe challenges will need to be disclosed to colleges earlier to discern the availability of services (say in the case of substantial executive function needs). For each college under consideration, students will determine the name of their admissions counselor. From that counselor, determine to whom a recent (no more than three years old) neurological-psychological/education testing evaluation report should be sent. Often that person is the Director of Learning Services. Send the report to each college you are considering and the college will respond as to whether or not the student can be accommodated. If you can be accommodated, then apply. If not, then do not apply. Keep your counselor informed.

Resources for Students with Learning Differences and their Families

Transitional Skills for Post Secondary Success by Teresa A. Citro

Editorial Reviews of Transitional Skills for Post Secondary Success:

"(This book) should be in the hands of every guidance counselor in this country and in every public library."
Suzanne Peyton, Exec. Dir. Mass Assoc. of Special Education Parent Advisory Councils

"(This book) will be of great help in the planning of one of life's most significant transitions."
Richard D. Lavoie, Former President, Riverview School

Colleges for Students with Learning Disabilities or ADD by Peterson's

Learning Disabilities Worldwide www.ldworldwide.org

Association of Higher Education and Disability
www.ahead.org

A great book for those with physical challenges:

The College and Career Success Bible for Those with Physical Disabilities
How to Transition from Motivated Student to Happily Employed Graduate

by Julia Nelson

Assignment: create a list of colleges to visit

 (This can be 5 to 20 colleges, if more, consider bringing what you have into your college counselor, for his or her review.)

* Your list *should* be balanced with: Likely schools, Target schools, and Reach schools.
* Also, factor in the cost of your colleges if you are applying for financial aid.

Teacher Recommendations

Ideally teacher recommendations address each hemisphere of the mind: sciences, languages and math as well as English, history and the humanities. Most of us are good at one or the other and two strong recommendations is the goal. Two recommendations from one side or the other is fine.

Do I need to have A's? No. Sometimes the best recommendations come from a teacher in a class in which you may have struggled at the beginning, maybe even earning C's at the mid-year, but through extra help, tutoring, and just hard work and perseverance, you performed better in the second half of the year. That can be a great recommendation!

It helps if recommendations are from teachers who like you.

Teachers in subjects close to your interest or major, if you have one, will help. In some cases, such as engineering, nursing, and other professional type programs, specific courses are often needed or sought and scrutinized. Higher grades in courses like Calculus and Biology may be needed. (Check with your admissions counselor, if you don't already know). Recommendations from those subject teachers will be weighted heavily. Engineering majors, for example, should seek a recommendation from teachers in physics and junior year math. Recommendations for art-related majors must come from the art department, plus one non-art subject teacher recommendation, if at all possible. Some art colleges look closely at English grades for example.

Try to pick recommendations from teachers who taught junior year, core courses. If needed, sophomore teachers can be used, but never freshman year teachers.

Normally, no more than two are needed.

Some faith-based colleges seek pastoral recommendations. These can come from youth group leaders. If necessary, you may ask an aunt, uncle or other adult that can speak to your spiritual journey, or, as a last option, ask a friend to write this one.

Some colleges ask for peer recommendations. Pick these carefully choosing a friend who is observant and a thoughtful writer may be a better recommendation than one from your best friend.

A Word on Extra Recommendations

Colleges, especially top colleges, require two teacher recommendations. These recommendations should describe a student's performance in class, preferably in one of your core courses: math science, history, foreign language and English.

However, one or two additional recommendations from teachers in non-core areas, coaches, campus ministers, employers, etc. would be appropriate if their recommendation could, in some way, distinguish you from other students - e.g. leadership, values, immersion trips, extraordinary talent in band, art, etc. In other words, this extra recommendation must address some aspect of you that is not in the recommendations from the core subject teachers.

Steps to Obtain Those Recommendations

1. Discuss your teacher options with your college counselor.

2. Agree on the two teachers you will ask for recommendations.

3. After class (tomorrow), ask the teacher: "Hi Mr. Smith, would you please write a letter of recommendation for me for college?" If a yes, then: "Thank you very much and what can I give you to help with it?"
4. Ask any coaches, pastors or any other writers the same question.

Learn the important terms necessary to navigate the admissions process

Early Decision

ED stands for Early Decision and it is binding, except if financial aid is insufficient. Therefore, if you are not applying for financial aid, the Early Decision is fully binding; you must attend if admitted. If you did apply for financial aid and it is not enough, call financial aid and respectfully ask for more. They may or may not increase the aid. Deadlines are most commonly November 1 (with a December 15 notification date) but can also be November 15 or another date. Some colleges have two rounds of ED. The second round of deadlines tends to be January 1 with a February 15 notification date.

It is strongly recommended that you perform at least two visits to an ED school in order to be sure that this college is the right one for you. Because this is binding, students may submit only one application using ED. If admitted under an ED program, you must email all other colleges where you have an application to withdraw it.

Early Action

EA stands for Early Action and includes the same dates as ED, but this is a non-binding application method. Students need to decide from all admission offers by May 1. Because EA is not binding, students may apply to as many EA colleges as they choose.

EA Modified or Single Choice Early Action means students may apply and hear back early from a college, but they can only apply early to one school.

There is also Modified or Restricted EA, limiting the number of EA applications

Regular Decision

Regular Decision means that there is an application deadline, commonly January 1, January 15, some deadlines in February and even dates in March. Notification from the colleges is expected April 1. This gives the student one month to decide which school they will attend before the May 1, the national deposit due date.

Rolling Admissions

Rolling Admissions refers to colleges reviewing applications and filling seats on a rolling basis. Once an application is complete, it is reviewed and notification occurs usually 3-4 weeks later. Seats can fill early, so although some of these may be probable, submit applications early (dates discussed later) to increase the chance of acceptance.

Instant Admission

This is very rare, but found in some states. Some colleges will routinely visit high schools, review transcripts and letters of recommendation or test scores in front of the student and will admit students on the spot. The other decision a student may hear during this meeting is a deferral (usually dependent upon additional senior year grades). There are no ID denials.

Types of Admissions Candidates

Standard Candidate

A standard admissions candidate is a student who does not fall into one of the categories below.

Recruited Candidate

A recruited athlete admissions candidate is a student who is being pursued by the college's Athletic Department. Formally this means athletic scholarships are being considered.

Underrepresented Candidate

An underrepresented candidate is a member of either an ethnic group or another minority division at a particular school. Note that on many campuses, a person of Asian descent is not commonly considered a minority student. This is due to the perception of the important role that education plays in Asian culture and to the perception that an admissions advantage is not needed. The prevalence of Asian students applying to colleges also makes this group less "unique" on the college campus.

Legacy Candidate

A legacy admissions candidate is a student whose parents or grandparents have attended the college. Aunts, uncles, brothers or sisters who have attended a college can help with admissions, but not as much as a legacy parent or grandparent. It can help if the college alumni have been active in some way, such as having held interviews for admissions or having been active college donators.

Stealth

A candidate that has never contacted the school, visited nor saw them at the high school visit. The first time the college learns about this applicant is when the application comes in to admissions. This is not a good status to have as most colleges will track your demonstrated interest.

Donor

A Donor admissions candidate is a candidate whose family has committed to donate usually large sums of money.

Types of Outcomes

Accept

You're in. Congratulations!

Deny

Usually bad news and once a decision is made, it is made, unless there is important information that was not submitted in error, like a higher SAT or ACT scores.

Deferred

Deferred (if EA/ED/modified)

If a student applied early, he or she can be accepted, denied, or deferred into the regular pool, usually because colleges like to see additional senior year grades. Keep your grades up. Very few colleges do not defer into the regular pool. For those schools, be sure you are near the top of their SAT test ranges if you are applying early.

Waitlisted

This occurs late in the process, April 1 of the senior year. It is by no means the end of the process. Notify your college counselor if this happens. There are tactics that can be discussed that can substantially increase the chance of being admitted from the waitlist. In this case, consider asking a professor or coach you met to help.

Now that you are empowered with knowledge, visit colleges!

The College Visit

The campus visit is probably the most important action a student can perform. It is kind of obvious that you would never want to attend a college for four years without ever having seen it, as websites can be deceiving and cannot portray the full college experience.

Once on campus, there is so much more than just touring that you will want to do.

Essentially you will want to become an anthropologist, that is, one who aims to understand a culture or a society based on pieces of information. During the college visit, ask yourself: "Can I see myself at this college for four years?"

Visit Overview

The best time to visit a college is when it is in session. Here is the challenge: many colleges are closed the same time that high schools are closed, such as during summer and winter breaks. Plan to visit local colleges within a two to three hour drive from your home on Saturdays (when the colleges are in session.) Colleges farther away from your home may need to be visited during high school spring break, as long as the colleges are also not on spring break.

Keep in mind that there are just so many hours in a day and that a proper college visit should take a full day. Although there can be very few students and professors on campus in the summer, sometimes that is the only time available.

Most colleges offer information sessions (usually lasting 45 minutes and held in the admissions office) and tours (usually one hour long, starting and ending at the admissions office.) Usually information sessions and tours are offered two to three times per day, so check the college website under admissions, before booking college trips.

Students should visit a minimum of three colleges and up to as many as ten or even fifteen. A recruited athlete may visit even more. Because these visits take time, you and your college counselor should select your visits carefully. Although visits can be spread out over time, most visits should be completed before the start of the senior year due to the demands of applications and essays throughout the fall. Some colleges offer interviews, and while information sessions and tours are public and often no reservation is needed, interviews must be scheduled in advance either via the college website or by telephone. Interviews will be covered in detail later.

Visit Planning

If you are visiting colleges in your junior year, consider making your initial list of visits more reach oriented, with possibly one likely college and at least one target-college. This is important because, if you like a reach college, you may want to visit it multiple times in order to gain more information for your applications.

Create Lists of Questions to Ask

Once you have prepared a list of colleges to visit, create lists of, questions to ask when on the visit. Take your time to complete these lists because the work you put in here will make it easier to further identify and clarify right fit colleges that are most likely to meet your needs.

Visit Questions can be split into three primary categories.

Category one- generic questions

These are generic and you will ask them of all colleges. These relate to things that are important to you. Category one includes questions such as the availability of substance-free/wellness/quiet dorms and the number of students in a particular club or organization that is important to you.

Category two- college questions

These are specific questions relevant to a particular college that may have surfaced in your research, such as the availability of an honors college and its admissions standards, or a question related to some statistic or academic program unique to a particular college. Your college counselor can help with these questions and some sample questions are listed later in this book.

Category three- person-specific questions

These questions are asked to someone specific at a college, such as a coach, a student, or a professor.

Remember, a full visit can take a whole day, so plan accordingly.

The Visit Day

Students must bring a notebook, a folder with copies of resumes, transcripts and a writing utensil. The notebook is used to write down your questions, and to place additional questions, concerns or notes from the visit day.
It will also be used for summary reflections of your experiences while at the college and meeting with staff.

<u>Dress</u> should be business casual. No ripped jeans! No sunglasses worn inside. This is not a club or a dance. This is serious business. Also wear comfortable walking shoes!

Boys wear khaki type pants, a collared shirt, either polo/Henley type or a button down shirt. Jacket (suit type, not a casual/baseball jacket) is preferred, especially for top colleges. No hats please.

<u>Important:</u> When students arrive in admissions (hopefully a few minutes before the tour or information session starts) ask the receptionist the name of the counselor assigned to the student's high school (occasionally they organize counselor assignments another way such as by last initial). Ask for your counselor's contact information. You will need the name, email, mailing address and telephone number of your admissions counselor.

After the information has been given to you, perhaps on a business card, ask if the counselor is available, and, if so, go in and introduce yourself. Basically, all you need to say is: "hi, I am from this high school, visiting and just wanted to say hello". At that time the counselor will strike up a quick conversation and then either say goodbye or invite you to their office for an impromptu interview. Don't worry you will be ready.

If the counselor is in that day, but temporarily out of his or her office, you should try back later. If the counselor is out for the day, simply email them when you are home and share your brief observations of the visit.

Keep this person's contact information and all other collected school materials for future use! **This person is critical in the application process.**

College's Information Session

Usually the information session takes place in a conference room. Sometimes there is a large table around which many sit, including the information provider. Other times the information session may be set up like a classroom with chairs instead of desks. Sometimes information sessions are held in auditoriums. In all cases, you must have a notebook ready and a pen in hand.

You do not have to write a thing. However, if the presenter says anything of interest or you think of a question that cannot be answered in that setting, jot down a few words to help you remember it. Generally, at an information session you get to sit, listen and ask a question or two.

If there are few people there, you may be asked general questions about your possible field of study or extracurricular activities or hobbies so they can direct the information session toward what they think you want to know.

The Campus Tour

If you arrive a bit late and find a tour group leaving the admissions building and about to start, just join it. Very important: be sure to sign in with admissions when the tour returns, although some large colleges may not have sign-ins.

Colleges take a special note of students who will demonstrate extra effort when learning about and or applying to a college. This is particularly true for many small and medium sized colleges, and those that have varied application requirements beyond the usual test scores and grade averages.

The tour will familiarize you with the college environment. Take note where buildings of interest are located. For example, if you like science, note where the science building is since you will want return to that building later. When you visit the dorms (usually they show you the nicest rooms), smell the air. If there is a pungent smell like the burning of a plant and it is 10 am, this is not a good sign. Are there piles of empty beer cans on Wednesday morning? Again, this is not good.

Is the library empty but students are ten deep around pinball machines in the student common, or vice versa?

If you love working on the Yearbook make sure the school you attend has a place for you on their yearbook staff. If you are at peace with the great outdoors make sure give special consideration to attending a school that has easy access to many activities outside.

If you are lucky enough to be the only family accompanied by a tour guide (rainy day?), you can ask the guide questions and the guide will tend to be more candid with you than with a crowd. Keep in mind, however, tour guides have been trained by, and work for, admissions (either volunteer or paid) and will rarely go off script to disclose weaknesses. You should ask tough questions and, fortunately, there are many other students on campus who will be more honest.

It is very important for the student to pick up a college newspaper, bundles are usually everywhere on campus. If lying around, pick up a few of the past issues. They are usually free and are goldmines of information. College students write them and write about what is important to students. Are any of these topics important to you? The college students are also brutally honest about the administration, campus crime, food, and other issues. Be sure to pick up these college newspapers! These papers are one of the key reasons to visit while colleges are in session. Sometimes they can be found online.

If you started in the morning, by this time it is either interview time or time to try the food at one of the dining halls. This dining room visit is important. Since you will eat this food for four years, and it better be good, or at least edible!

Imagine expanding your comfort zone and ask questions of the people you randomly see and or meet. If you see students sitting alone, feel free to approach them, just as you would a professor. After introducing yourself as a high school student considering applying to their school they will likely be very helpful and informative.

At this point in your visit, if you have followed the above sequence of events, you know a bit about the college, you ate some (hopefully) good food and you were entertained by an information session host and tour guide. Now you must do a little work.

You must visit professors and get their contact information in the event that you have follow-up questions (or possibly need it for the application). Ask them some of the questions listed at the end of this book. If you are not sure about majors but have two or three interests, meet a professor from each area of interest. If you are studying drama, meet a drama professor or a department chair and ask questions. Also, if you are an athlete, visit the coach or assistant coach and ask questions, in addition to professors. Visit with students as discussed earlier, if you can. Parents should stop by the financial aid department and inquire about any scholarship and any other information that may not be on the web site.

This is where you have the choice to go the extra mile to make sure a college is right and or not for you. Find a professor in his or her office and introduce yourself as a high school student, considering the college. Ask if the professor has a few minutes for a couple of questions?

Before leaving a discussion with a professor you may choose to ask that person for any other people they suggest you contact for more information and given your interests. They may give you a student club leader's name or a head of a department. For possible later research and contact, write the person's name.

Send a Thank You card to this professor and or any other person who goes out of their way to help you.

Classrooms

Eavesdrop on a classroom, or sit in on one, usually arranged through admissions.

While in the academic building visiting professors, eavesdrop on a classroom, listening for a minute where you cannot be seen. Are the students participating? Is the professor respectful? When you walk by and look in, are students in the back awake?

Admissions can sometimes arrange for you to sit in on a class, but this takes some time and can wait until April, after you have been admitted and have more time.

Other Places to Visit

You may also want to go back to the dorms and see if you can bypass security. Don't worry; security won't get you in trouble. If you can bypass security, either security is sleeping or a door is propped open; either is bad, because someone unauthorized also may be able to get in.

Be sure to read bulletin boards! They give you a great idea of what is going on in the local area and what students and professors are thinking and doing.

At this point, given you and your family's time and motivation, visit the career office or placement office.

Obtain a feel for the office while asking some questions. Keep in mind that after spending four plus years and lots of money and time you want to know you will be getting a job for your efforts!

Ask to speak with a counselor. With that person, find out whether students are often offered jobs before they graduate?

What businesses are recruiting students at that school each year?
(If widely respected organizations are hiring school X's graduates consider this a good thing. If students are not being recruited by leading companies and or students are finding themselves out of work for a year after graduation, this may draw red flags for you to further research.)

What are the salaries ranges of students who leave the school?

Will the college help you find a job?

Buyer beware, If a school is or is not training marketable people you want to know this before you attend the college.

Fantastic You're Done!

Now take a moment to reflect:

Did you have fun? Did the school seem exciting or boring or somewhere in between? Will you find people on campus to learn with and from in classes and outside? Was it a Good fit for you? Extracurriculars?

That night, or in the car or on your way to the next hotel or college, students must jot down notes about each college. Write points you liked best and least about each college in addition to general observations. This is so critical because after visiting two to three colleges, all colleges start to look and sound alike. You can also look through the "propaganda" picked up in admissions and file it for future reference.

Powerful Business Etiquette

After completing a college visit, you must send a thank you card to each person who spent time with you.

Tip: Buy and keep readily accessible a box of thank you cards and stamps, for the writing of notes to all of the people who take any special time to support you in your process.

Mailing addresses are located on saved business cards; emails are not as good for this.

The note can be simple:

Sample Thank You Note

> *Dear Admissions interviewer or Counselor (first name) or Professor or Coach (last name),*
>
> *Thank you for spending time with me on (name the weekday and date).*
>
> *I enjoyed learning more about___, __, and ____.*
>
> *Thanks again for your time.*
>
> *Sincerely,*
>
> (Sign your first and last name, legibly, even if making it legible is not your normal signature.)
>
> (Print under your name, your high school, the town in which it is located, the state and your email address.)

Visit Checklists

Pre-Visit Checklist

(To be on top of your game as well as avoid unnecessary confusion and or anxiety, use this checklist before attending each college visit)

-Bring a pen, notebook, folder, camera, and a copy of the campus map (find on website)

-Check times on web site for tour and information session, under admissions and check the college academic calendar to be sure they are open.

-Make a special note of the people and places you want to visit before leaving for the day.

-Book an interview (if offered)

-Read interview part of this book

-Research college academics, clubs and crimes web site (for questions to ask admissions, a professor of interest, or the tour guide)

-Write up generic and college specific questions

-Bring copies of your academic transcript and resume

-Read THE COLLEGE VISIT section of this book again.

The Visit Checklist

(Use this checklist the day of the visit)

-Take the admissions tour, interview and information session--be sure they know you are there by signing in.

-Meet your admissions counselor, or at the very least, obtain his/her contact information.

-Eat the food

-Meet professors

-Meet students

-Pickup college newspaper

-Ask questions from list

-Visit the placement or career office, dorms, student center, and all other locations of interest

-If applicable to you, visit the athletic facility or the art department.

Post-Visit Checklist

Be organized by completing this checklist.

-Reflect on your visit and notes. A page or so of notes for each college is great. (These will be helpful later in the process when details become fuzzy!)

-As soon as possible, and before you forget, send thank you cards (not emails) to interviewers, professors, coaches and anyone in admissions who spent time with you.

-Process your thoughts and feelings with family, friends, and your college counselor after a group of college visits.

-Place all of the materials you take from a school and or receive in the mail into a filing system of your choice. A simple manila folder will work labeled with the name of each college.

A typical college visit schedule:

8:45	Check-in at admissions office
9:00	Guided campus tour
10:00	Information session
12:00	Interview
1:00	Dining hall lunch
1:30	Independent touring and questioning
4:00	Leave campus
4:30	Write journal notes, download any photos and organize materials gathered

College Preparation Specific to Artists

Additional steps need to be addressed when applying for an art major in college.

Visual Arts

As early as the end of sophomore year and no later than the middle of junior year, notify your high school art department of your college major intention. An art teacher should help you assemble the required portfolio. Let your college counselor know if he or she is not yet aware. Start creating and saving your art works as early as possible in your high school years. Pre-high school, work is rarely applicable.

Each college will have specific portfolio requirements and portfolio review dates. Check each of the requirements on the college web sites and discuss them with your high school art faculty. Be sure you keep review dates. Remind your teachers of them so both of you are working toward the same goal.

Performing Arts

Auditions are required. See your instrumental, vocal or composition teachers at your high school for assistance. See theatre teachers and ask for audition help if you plan to pursue theatre. College web sites have specific audition requirements and audition dates. It is the student's responsibility to manage audition. Keep your high school teachers aware of these dates and requirements as well. They may be available to help students rehearse and otherwise prepare for auditions and entrance exams. Give your college counselor, as appropriate, those dates as well.

A Word on Audition DVDs

For both the performing and visual arts, be mindful of media requirements. If an audition DVD for a theatre, music, or film major is required, start preparing it in the junior year. Preparations include selecting pieces, editing, compiling and copying the DVD. This can be expensive and time consuming. Start early and try to find friends or family members who may have video edit experience in order to keep costs down. Also be prepared to add to the DVD any pieces that may be created in the summer before the senior year or in the fall of senior year.

College Preparation for Students with Special Academic Considerations

Art/Architecture

Begin assembling your portfolio no later than January of the junior year with the help of your art teacher. Check architecture college websites for specific requirements.

Service Academies: US Naval Academy, US Air Force Academy, US Military Academy at West Point, US Coast Guard Academy, US Merchant Marine Academies

Service academies have very specific admissions requirements including congressional nominations and physical fitness tests. Review these on their websites as soon as possible. Look for their summer programs which often are the first step in the admissions process which also provide a glimpse into what a service academy life is like. Begin discussing these options with your college counselor January of junior year.

Nursing, Physical Therapy, Occupational Therapy and Other Health Majors

These majors tend to have only a specific number of seats in a class due to the unique nature of their labs or popularity in the case of business. Be sure that your scores are at least in the colleges' mean SAT/ACT statistics and be sure that you apply early in the admit season. Some colleges seek much higher than the mean test scores for these majors. Ask you admissions counselor.

Sample questions to ask most people on campus

These can be used generically, with all colleges. Add your own particular questions.

What do students like the best about this college?

What do students say they like least?

Other than changing majors, what is the most common reason a student transfers out?

Academically, are there any new majors or departments planned?

Questions in this category help gain a sense of where the college is going academically.

It is nice to see that colleges are growing in areas interesting to you, If they are not beware of opportunities for future struggles and mismatches at that school.

Student Life Questions

Questions to ask admissions officers

Are there dorms that are commonly referred to as substance free/wellness/quiet/chemical free?

The benefit of these is huge. Often times they are the nicest and newest dorms. Also, common charges billed to all dorm residents at the end of the year due to vandalism, usually fueled by substance abuses, can be hundreds of dollars. Lastly, attending parties are a normal part of college life, but do you really want the noise, mess, and frequent "accidents" (read: vomit) to happen in your dorm bed, room or outside your door, 24/7?

How many students regularly attend "the club" and how often do they meet?

"The club" is any interest you have now or expect to explore. In college there are often clubs for everything: Photography, Yoga, Religious beliefs, Pilates, Outdoor Activities, A Cappella, you name it. But the club is only as good as the number of people engaged in the activity, and this is why this question is so important. The Office of Student Life should have the answer or the college website. If not, at least Student Life will have email addresses for club presidents who will know the answers.

Are there college-wide, or other activities that do not include drinking? If so, what are they?

Academic Questions

To ask admissions counselors, professors and or students

Is there an honors college or honors program?

This is an especially important question for any larger colleges and universities you are considering. It is also important for financially concerned families, since the student may be eligible for merit aid.

Are there any college-wide graduation requirements such as a thesis or comprehensive exam?

You should review the college catalog for academic programs of interest.

Review course titles both in the major field of concentration and also in any core requirements. This review could generate another question or two. These questions are then usually best asked of a department professor.

Are there teaching assistants?

You want to be taught by a professor, rather than a teaching assistant, because professors know the real life applications of theory that most teaching assistants do not know.

How available are professors outside of class?

What is the quality of academic advising? This is important because student majors can be decided in college.

May I have a list of research performed by undergraduates that has been published in a scholarly journal?

Many many colleges tout research opportunities available, but how significant are they? Research could be you cleaning beakers, or performing real research with a professor that will be published.

Is the engineering program ABET accredited? Is the business program AACSB accredited?

Admissions Questions

To ask admissions representatives or professors

Are students admitted to the university, the college/school, or to the major?

And are potential major (s) competitive (such as nursing, business and engineering)?

Are there any majors that have higher admissions standards than another?

This is a great way to see if the college is admitting to the major, as opposed to the overall college. It will help confirm one way or another if a college is a probable, a target, or a reach school.

Determine if there are unique admissions requirements for your possible major(s).

Some colleges look to certain course grades or subject test scores for these majors.

Research which early program the school currently has, if any (EA, ED, etc), and ask if they plan to continue to use it your senior year. Ask if they defer into the regular pool any early applications that are borderline. A few colleges just admit or deny from the early pool.

Research the crime website to see if there is anything to ask about (later in book).

How many students are in the largest class? How many classes are of that size? How many classes are over 25 or 30 students? 50? This is very important because the class sizes should match your preferred learning style as much as possible. If you prefer lecture classes/notes then larger classes will suit you.
If you prefer discussion classes, then smaller classes will facilitate this.

Are there living/learning communities where they house students together with the same majors?

Remember: These are great questions to ask and college admission officers will make mental notes that they will write down after you leave. They too are anthropologists and a student who asks thoughtful questions in admissions will most likely ask thoughtful questions in the classroom, thus pleasing professors and admissions alike.

Other Questions

Questions to ask professors and/or career services, also known at some colleges as the Career Center

In my area(s) of interest, what proportion of graduates goes directly into the job market versus directly to graduate school?

Which grad schools do they commonly attend?

Which employers commonly hire them?

What are the average salaries?

Questions for Actors

What courses do you offer for theatre majors?

Do you subscribe to a particular method of training actors?

Do students need to apply separately for the theatre program at this school, or do they apply to the school first and then audition for the theatre program once they begin attending the school?

Will audition requirements change for next year? (Check website for existing requirements first.)

Do students need to be theatre majors and/or audition for a school theatre company in order to be a part of the casting pool for school productions? Or are auditions open to all students?

Can non-theatre majors realistically hope to get significant roles?

Can all theatre majors realistically expect to get significant roles before they graduate?

What have some of your recent productions been? Why were those productions chosen?

What do you hope to see from an actor in an audition?

Questions for Musicians

Are the audition requirements next year expected to be the same or similar to those of the current year? (Check the website first)

What are the audition dates? (Again, check website first)

What are the application requirements/deadlines?

What is the nature of music program and is it in line with your musical goals? (I.e. improvisational or classical or contemporary music instruction)

Question to ask yourself

Are there any pre-college programs to help with admissions, such as private lessons? Coaching? High school electives or directed studies?

Questions for Visual Artists

What scholarship opportunities are there for foreign travel and study?

What is the quality of current student and faculty visual artwork like, and is it work that you respect and can learn from? Are you inspired by what you see?

What space is available for studio work for freshman though to the senior year?

What is the availability of work and studio space outside a particular medium to each student? Example: can a student use the ceramics studio if they are a painter?

How will the school assist me in finding a job?

Is there an academic support system in place?

What is the availability of the professor to the student outside of class?

College Interview

Interviews are a great way for colleges to get to know you and for you to get to know them.

Most people feel uncomfortable during their first few interviews in any process, whether it is for college, an internship, or a job. Once you have completed your first one or two interviews, they become much easier, more comfortable as you master the skill.

Two Types of Interviews:

1. Evaluative: Consider the job interview, these meetings tend to be evaluative in nature as they are evaluating based on your qualifications for the responsibilities of the position.

2. Informative: On the other hand, people who sell time-shares tend to hold informative interviews; they primarily talk about their business offerings without evaluating.

College admissions interviews tend to be a bit of both - evaluative and informative.

Basic Interview Rules

1. Always have paper, pad or notebook, some questions, and a writing utensil.

2. Be sure not to ask questions that are in the view book or easily found on the website

3. Be confident and discuss your strengths, hobbies and interests enthusiastically.

4. Shake hands with eye contact before and after

5. Be prepared to answer the following questions an admissions officer is likely to ask of you at an interview

6. Dress for success!

7. Bring copies of your **resume and transcript.**

8. Prepare for your interviews by reading this again.

9. Wait to be seated

10. Collect the interviewer's contact information and always write thank you notes!

Mock Interview Exercise

Practice the skill of interviewing. Doing so will help you to be ready for both the planned or impromptu college admissions interview.

How?

With an adult, or friend if in class, choose several questions from the following list.

For three minutes, the interviewer will ask questions of the interviewee.

The interviewer will answer them as best as possible.

If with a friend, after the three minutes is up switch roles and repeat the exercise.

Both should experience what it feels like and know that feeling uncomfortable and unsure is normal.

Afterwards, give feedback to your partner and know that the more this skill is practiced the easier it becomes.

Scheduling an Interview

If you and your counselor decide that an interview is in your best interest, call the admissions office to organize a meeting. Request a meeting day for when you are already visiting the college.

Alternatively, some colleges may have an alumnus meet you at a Starbucks or some other public place. Regardless of location, your interview preparation is the same.

Sample interview questions

Here are some questions commonly asked. Practice and be able to answer each of them.

1. What do you see yourself doing five years from now?

2. Do you have an interest in a specific major? Why?

3. What are your career and professional goals?

4. What do you consider to be your greatest strengths and weaknesses?

5. How would you describe yourself?

6. What motivates you to put forth your greatest effort?

7. How has your high school experience prepared you for college? Would you do anything differently?

8. How do you determine or evaluate success?

9. What two or three accomplishments have given you the most satisfaction?

10. Describe your most rewarding high school experience.

11. What interests you about our college?

12. Do you think that your grades are a good indication of your academic achievements?

13. What have you learned from your participation in extra-curricular activities?

14. How do you work under pressure?

15. In what part-time or summer jobs/activities have you been most interested? Why?

16. What major problem have you encountered and how did you deal with it?

17. What have you learned from your mistakes?

18. How do you spend your spare time? What are your hobbies?

19. What men and women have influenced your life the most and why?

20. What paper did you write last year that impacted you the most, and why?

Introduction to the college application essay

Colleges consider the importance of the essay differently. In all cases, the essay should be well written, grammatically correct, and should be revealing about you. The college essay is the only opportunity you have to influence the process exclusively yourself. It is the one element of the application over which you have complete control.

The essay must always reflect much about what makes you "you." **The more revealing the essay is about you, the better it will be to Admissions Counselors.** Beware of too many "fingerprints" of people helping you because your "voice" should be clearly heard. While you want the essay to be well written, it must reflect you and your thoughts. Consider general criticisms or suggestions but beware of editors who make wholesale changes or too many word substitutions. Those may dilute your message and your voice. Your voice must come through.

Essay Types

There are at least four types of essay questions (listed below) and two types of lengths (short answer 150-250 words, and long answer 300-600 words.)

Long Essays

Self-revealing
This is by far the most common question encountered. This essay must be entirely about you, with little reference to the "frame" or topic of your portrait. This is not a creative writing or literary analysis; descriptive writing is **not** the goal, self-revealing writing is the goal.

Factual
Some may provide a historical fact or quote and seek your response to it. Here they want to know if you can be creative yet professional in your writing. These question types also measure breadth and depth of thought.

Creative
These questions can be entirely off the wall and again seek insight into your creativity and your professional writing techniques.

The above three essay types (self-revealing, factual, and creative) tend to be longer and the way to write them is discussed below, under Essay Procedures.

Short Essays

They tend to be short in length, 150-250 words and often the topics are either, "Why Us?" or "Why that?"

The "Why Us" question is seeking the answer to why you want to attend that particular college. This is an important one. Schools may feel that you are a match; however they want to know why **you** may think that you are a match. They ask you this question to find out if you have done your research.

This type of essay is typically easier because 'Why Us?" or "Why that?" essays are short!

For "Why Us?" essays, gather your notes from your visits.

Consider the curriculum and programs: Consider these either in the way they are delivered or by their content. Do they make sense for your ambitions? How does college x offering from college y? You need to know that and tell college x what excites you about their offerings.

Consider the people: Get a sense of the people you met: the admissions people, the students and the professors, ideally all three. How do you feel about them?

Consider your senses: How were the food, the air, and the campus vistas? How did you feel, emotionally? Was there the "heart factor", that is, you just loved It there?

In all three of these considerations write a sentence or two addressing each one, or address just the ones that resonate with you.

For essay questions that may ask you to write about why you chose a particular interest or hobby, merely write from the heart (see below for further guidelines on how to begin). Then edit carefully to use only the very best words, since so few are required.

Read your draft, revise and revise it again before showing it to others. You should be prepared to go through many more revisions. Try not to get frustrated. Quality writing always takes frequent, careful revision and takes time. Ask adults who you think are good writers to review your drafts. Take risks with your writing and topics but remember your essay must reveal who you are. Once you are happy with the quality of your final drafts, show essays to your college counselor.

Writing the College Application Essay (Five Steps)

Follow these essay procedures to write long and short essays

First Step: Pick your theme

Pick a theme that is interesting to you, ignore the prompt for now. The essay must ultimately describe who you are, touching upon your values, strengths, weaknesses and personality characteristics.

Think about your:

Values

Strengths/weaknesses

Likes/dislikes

Ambitions/hobbies

Favorite reading materials/movies

Favorite lectures/classes

Favorite people/relatives

Also consider:

Who or what has shaped you the most into who you are today?

Give specific examples of who you are and how you have changed or developed as a result of your life experiences and people you know.

Second Step: Start writing free form

That is, write freely whatever comes to mind as you ponder this list. Use pages and pages of a pad, and take time.

Then, a day later, read it again. Can you add to your random thoughts?

Another day later, read your thoughts again, this time to look for a theme of either a Topic or the way in which you want to present yourself.

Third Step: Create an outline or go right to drafting

Show this to your counselor, if you have one, to make sure you are on the right track

Fourth Step: Begin drafting

Write a first draft.

Put it away for a day or more.

Read it again and now be sure it answer the essay question or prompt. Re-write it choosing your words more carefully. It is important to place yourself as an outsider unfamiliar with you and your draft. Ask yourself if the writing clearly describes the points you wish to make.

Draft again and consider showing it to someone who is a good writer. Beware of major, wholesale changes. Your voice must come through.

Draft again with any changes that you like.

Read it aloud. Does it sound like you? Draft again.

Fifth Step: Show a final draft to your college counselor

For any necessary adjustments prior to the final edits

Essay Writing Summary

Think of what makes you who you are and be revealing. Start writing and do not worry about the prompt early on.

Start to think about self-revealing college essays in the spring of your junior year.

By the summer before senior year, have your applications in hand so you know exactly the questions that need to be answered.

Have all your essay final drafts ready to show your college counselor by the start of your senior year, at the latest.

Part II Senior year: College Applications

Review any EA or ED Strategies

If ED is considered, see if one last visit and perhaps an overnight can be arranged in the fall (well before the deadline). There are many ways to do this, contact: a future teammate, coach, high school alumni from the last year or so, a club president or religiously affiliated (see club rosters online) member.

If you are a DIII athlete, consider updating your resume with summer activities and junior year-end GPA, and seek a "pre-admit" read by admissions, if the college coach will do it. Many do. In this way, especially if you are torn between two or three top ED colleges,
knowing which college will give the nod(s) yes is important as only one ED application is permitted.

Be prepared to commit to one school at this time. Many coaches make it a quid pro quo for the information from admissions. In other words, if the coach is going to say that it is likely that you will be admitted, then you have 24 hours to advise the coach if you will indeed apply ED and then, of course, attend. So be sure that this is the school for you. Be prepared to tell your college counselor about the curriculum (proof you know the college well). For example, do they have a senior capstone event such as a comprehensive exam or a senior thesis? You need to know this before you decide to attend any college.

Review College Lists

Questions to consider:

On a scale of one to ten, ten being the highest, how secure are you with your choices of colleges on your list?

What do you need to do, if anything, to be more secure?

Do you have plans to visit or re-visit any colleges?

Last Time to Revisit SAT/ACT Tests

And you thought you were done with these! Well you can be. But, if you are reaching for a college with a test mid range above your best scores, then consider how badly you want it and consider taking the test one more time. Youth brain development continues at a rapid pace, plus, by this point you have had a couple more months of reading and schooling to improve.

Senior Year Performance Goals

Important! You must keep these early senior year grades up. Colleges put much weight on the senior year and expect it to remain strong throughout the year. First semester grades can make or break a hard worked admission strategy. Don't blow it.

<u>General College Application, Strategies & Mechanics</u>

Four major components to the college application

(There are more parts if you are an artist, athlete, individual with an IEP or Section 504, and or a service academy candidate.)

1. The Application

2. Teacher Recommendations

3. Transcript/ guidance letter, secondary school report and profile

4. SAT/ACT scores sent via the Internet directly to colleges, by the student

Step #1 Open a commonapp.org account

If the commonapp is being used by one of the colleges you are considering, establish an account at www.commonapp.org

If the college does not take the commpnapp, establish an account at your colleges' websites.

There is also the Coalition Application, the Universal Application and the HBCU Application; the following guidelines can be used for all applications as well.

General Application Rules

Read instructions carefully!

Be sure essays answer the question or prompt and are revealing about you.

Never abbreviate, except where you must for space limitations or formal state abbreviations.

Proofread everything.

The Common Application, Strategies and Mechanics

Specific Application Tips (Particular Attention Given to the Common Application)

Naviance is used to send documents to colleges so no teacher recommendation information should be input into the common application.

Mid-year grades will be sent as you request them and as advised by your high school college counselor.

Final Report can be ignored for now as the high school automatically sends out your final transcript to the one college that you choose to attend.

Do any of your colleges use the commonapp? If so, set it up and start the application asap.

Setup a commonapp account on
www.commonapp.org

Common Application Tips

Language Proficiency: Generally if you have taken just 2 years of a language it would be difficult to be proficient. After completing three years you are nearing proficiency which means you can be proficient in 2 languages (English of course being the first). List them.

Fee Waivers: If you were offered a test fee waiver last year (SAT or ACT), then see your counselor and indicate yes, you will use a fee waiver.

Family Information: You will need employer info, college info and that of your siblings as well to complete this section.

Testing: Only indicate the tests that you will send. If you took both ACT and SAT, just indicate the test with the better result.

Activities: Only indicate those which you have attended with some regularity. Indicate what you derived, how you grew, what you got out of it. Do not just indicate what you did because that is normally obvious to the reader.

Writing: In addition to the main essay, you can and should write an additional one under Additional Information. Also be sure to review the essays that might exist as a supplement (seen under the My Colleges tab). Show these to your high school college counselor.

FERPA Waiver (under My Colleges tab): Must be completed and can only be completed once the Education part of the commonapp is complete (completed sections earn a green check mark).

Application Tips (a walk through the Common Application)

The following explains things to know and to look out for when completing a college applications. Many students use the common application so it is that format that is followed here.

On all applications, read the instructions very carefully!

When Colleges Come to High School

High schools are privileged to have colleges interested in visiting. Counselors often meet with the reps to learn about the colleges and to teach the colleges about the high school.

Students benefit as it is yet another opportunity to show interest, a very important part of the process which was discussed earlier in the book.

If they are visiting when you have a class, you must check in with the class teacher for permission to attend the college session. This is not guaranteed.

You must come to these visits with paper and pen/pencil in hand.

Top 5 Ways to Impress an Admissions Officer

By Liluye Jhala, ApplyWise counselor (formerly with Brown University)

It's the start of another busy fall semester. If you are a junior or senior, you probably already know that this is the time of year when college representatives are in your hometown visiting your high school, having evening receptions and attending local college fairs. These are all excellent ways to get information without having to visit the campus. It is also an opportunity to make a great impression on the admissions officer who may be evaluating your college application in a few short months.

As a former admissions officer at Brown, I know how engaging it is to meet students in their schools or hometowns. While the sheer volume of students could be overwhelming, it was always refreshing to meet someone who was enthusiastic, sincere and knowledgeable about Brown. Even after weeks away from home, I came back to Providence remembering a handful of students who made a positive impression on me. Here are my top five tips for making yourself a memorable candidate to any visiting admissions officer.

1. Be five minutes early

After you've decided which colleges you'd like to get to know better, plan ahead and try to get there early. If you are there first, you might have the opportunity to spend one-on-one time with the admissions officer. If it's a presentation, get a good seat close to the officer and take that time to introduce yourself. If it's a college fair, try to be one of the first individuals to speak with the admissions officer.

2. Dress (and behave) to impress

At the end of one of my typical presentations to a classroom of 150 students, most dressed very casually, I wandered to the back of the room and wound up chatting with a soft-spoken man in a suit. He followed every word I said and I assumed he was a teacher. At the end of our discussion, though, he thanked me for my talk and asked for my e-mail address. His whole presentation really made him stand out from his classmates. Remember, it's your job to make a positive impression. So, dress well and speak intelligently. You'll not only impress the admissions officer, but your classmates and teachers as well.

3. Ask thoughtful questions

Do your research on each college before they visit. You should be prepared not only to ask the admissions officer a few questions yourself, but to be asked some basic questions in return. Rest assured that unless it is a formal interview, the admissions officer is not interviewing you and, consequently, you probably will not be forced to speak on your greatest disappointments or academic hurdles during your very brief time together. However, you might want to have tentative responses to these very common questions:

1. What first drew you to this school?

2. What are your academic interests?

3. Why do you want to attend?

4. What do you do for fun?

5. What books do you read for fun?

Remember, be as specific as possible. The first and second questions are similar; the difference, however, is that the second question asks you to define what exactly makes a particular school special (i.e., the New Curriculum at Brown). Your response to the first question, however, could be based upon your own personal experience with a school (i.e., "It was so beautiful and I just loved the small community.") Also, be sure to include why a particular feature is appealing to you. The admissions officer is, after all, trying to get to know you as a person. Be honest.

For your part, ask the admissions officer a few qualitative, not quantitative, questions. A quantitative question might be about Brown's average SAT score, an answer to which you could easily find on Brown's Web site or in any college guidebook. As a matter of fact, before you attend any kind of university function for prospective students, you should already know the following about the school:

1. Required tests and courses. Do you have to take SAT II subject tests or four years of a foreign language?

2. The school's general curriculum and grading basics. A university may offer a range from a core curriculum to an open curriculum to a Great Books program. Also, familiarize yourself with the university's grading system.

3. Their current admission stats: the academic and standardized test averages of admitted students (i.e., the mean class rank, GPA, SAT, etc.).

4. The majors, minors or concentrations offered. After all, you cannot study Egyptology everywhere.

5. Their financial aid and/or work-study programs.

Financial aid

Students should involve their parents at this point, if not already, and share this section.

For those who qualify, financial aid is available from the colleges themselves, as well as from government entities, philanthropic organizations and businesses.

Student loans and campus work-study programs round-out typical financial aid awards. For college and government aid, student loans and work-study funds, all colleges require at least one of the following applications:

> **1) CSS Profile: Available online from Collegeboard.com and costs a small fee to file and another for each college to receive it.**
>
> **2) Free Application for Federal Student Aid (FAFSA): www.fafsa.ed.gov**
>
> **3) College's own financial aid application**

Some colleges require all three forms. Parents must contact each college, or check the websites of each college, to find out which forms must be filed.

The FAFSA can, and should, be completed immediately after October 1. Parents can import financial data from the Internal Revenue Service to make the process easier for them.

Mind the deadlines initially and mind them **each year** because financial aid, while usually renewed, must be applied for each year.

Missing deadlines can substantially reduce awards.

Private scholarships and search engines
Private scholarship are those from companies such as GM or USPS and philanthropic organizations like the Elks Lodge. Local philanthropic scholarship applications, if any, are often found in the high school counseling office; be sure to ask. Also check the town hall and local library as sometimes the notices or applications are found there.

Scholarships from private organizations can be found but are rare despite claims.

Fastweb.com is the web site that allows the student/family to answer a questionnaire seeking data on such areas as ethnicity, academic interest or major and even left-handedness (yes there are scholarships for left handed people).

Once the answers are given, fastweb.com in theory scans all other scholarship websites and emails you with information regarding the scholarships you may be eligible for. Check the details and if viable… i.e. they matched you properly to your answers or the requirements are not too onerous, (such as a 1000 word essay for a $50 scholarship), then apply.

These sites may help you find and apply for scholarships.

Searching for scholarships may however take a large amount of time to complete. Keep this step as a lower priority as compared to the other essential application and financial tasks.

As you do have time, explore the below sites.

http://www.fastweb.com Great scholarship search engine, also has a college search engine

http://www.scholarshipamerica.org Another scholarship search engine

http://www.scholarships.com This is a great site for exploring many different privately ` available scholarships

http://www.finaid.com Another site for exploring private aid and scholarships

http://yahoo.com/education/financial_aid Good resource for other financial aid web sites

Government websites

http://www.fafsa.ed.gov This is the government's web page for Federal Application for Free Student Aid

http://www.teri.org Stands for The Educational Resource Institute- a source for aid

http://www.nelliemae.org Student loan programs

http://www.salliemae.com More information regarding student loans

http://216.74.11.178 This is a strange URL for MOLIS, which is Minority Online Information System, a web site for financial aid as well as other resources

Transitioning to College

What will you need to know?

Introduction

Ever since elementary school you have been accumulating knowledge. Initially it may have felt as if it was forced upon you, but by now, more often than not, you find yourself seeking the education to meet *your* goals.

Yet, too many college students jeopardize their experience and cripple, delay or even kill their goals and dreams. For this reason, it is worth considering issues related to transitioning into college life and issues related to college health. The implications of both can have a lifelong impact.

The college experience can be one of the best in your life, due substantially to issues discussed here and decisions you either have made or will shortly make.

Senior Year Before You Go

Spring:

Be smart at graduation parties. You worked hard to earn admissions to college and your future looks bright. Be sure to keep it that way!

Colleges will mail a **residence hall** questionnaire either in the spring or early summer. Sometimes an online link is provided. Some students will answer these questions based on the roommate they want rather than who they really are. Be honest and you will increase the odds of a good roommate match.

Tips: Make mature decisions at graduation parties.
Roommate Survey - Be honest in your answers.

Summer

You just graduated! Now, keep in mind that change is hard for everyone, especially those not leaving, such as your family unit: siblings and parents. Behaviors on everyone's part can be unusual as a new family dynamic is forming. Just be prepared for this and be understanding. Much grace is required.

Tip: Be patient and tolerant of unusual behaviors around the home.

Packing for College

Mark your valuables with a unique mark or a driver's license number, not a social security number. Photograph this mark and the valuable items. Keep the photos in an email to yourself. The camera or phone could be stolen.
Also in an email, keep a list of valuable items with model numbers and serial numbers. This makes it easier for insurance company reimbursement.

Tip: Mark and list all valuable items before you pack.

The First Days and Weeks of College

What to be aware of in those initial weeks

Move-In Day

You may be thinking, "Wow! Though we have spoken a few times over the summer to discuss what each was bringing, I can't believe it is actually time to meet my roommates, and to start a new life!"

This might seem silly, but a theft could ruin the first day. Be sure to lock your car and dorm room while you are unloading belongings. Especially in urban environments where it is harder to identify who belongs there; thieves target move-in day as a time to make a lot of money. Even in locked cars, do not leave valuables in view this especially includes laptops, cell phones and mp3 players.

Tip: Beware of move-in day thieves

First Days

College orientation is typically a few days in July or August or maybe the days just prior to starting classes. Orientation is a great place to meet new friends and to learn how the college operates. Avoid the temptation to skip it as some of your new friends may suggest. Many colleges have extensive orientation activities that can span days or weeks. Enjoy them; you will make new friends there. Know that some orientations can try to indoctrinate you into the college's worldview. **It is important to both be tolerant of others' views and to be sure to remain true to who you are and true to your values.**

Tip: Be sure to attend orientation! Watch for indoctrination.

First Weeks

"College, overall, is cool, yet the roommate is questionable".

Give roommate relations time to gel. Sometimes relations are easily forged, yet other times it can take weeks. Do not give up too early and know that some friendships take time. Again be tolerant, but do not compromise your values.

If your roommate is taking or selling drugs, immediately, and before things get worse, tell the Resident Assistant (RA) or someone else in charge. Seriously consider telling the RA that you would like a room change and that you are in no way interested in this activity. This is important to you because a roommate that openly exposes his illegal activities may not hesitate to drag you down in front of others. Often colleges have a "Zero Tolerance" policy when it comes to drugs. If caught around drugs in the dorm you will likely be kicked out of the dorms and possibly expelled from college.

Tips: Give roommate relations time to gel, but do not compromise your values. Take illegal activities in your room very seriously, you could get caught up in something regrettable.

Focus on healthy relationships and academics.

Emotional and Psychological Safety

In General

Decide now what your "college experience" will be, after all, you are in charge. Be aware that the media's portrayal of the college experience and know that is not what everyone is seeking.

You are able to make the college experience exactly what you want. This is huge, because it can vary so widely. Reinvent yourself day one if there are study habits or other behaviors that you want to change. You are, in a way, starting over, which is hard to do later in life!

The ages of 18-22 are critical in human development terms. Higher level thinking abilities are being formed as brain physiology is nearing completion.

While the finishing touches are being applied to your mind, sudden independence is thrust upon college-age students. Life-changing decisions are being made while life is still being discerned.

Tip: The college-experience forces a range of choices on students when you are not always prepared to make the wisest ones. **There make important decisions carefully. Role play in your mind responses to invitations you don't want. Role playing in your mind substantially increases the chance you will stay strong and thrive.**

Homesickness

Homesickness is something to consider, even for the most adventurous students.

With so much newness at college how could it be avoided? The new people, scents, tastes, and sleeping arrangements... it is no wonder that homesickness is common. At times, call home, but maybe not too frequently, as this can prolong feelings of discomfort and needs for escape.

If possible, avoid going home in the first month due to homesickness. Friendships are being forged during the early weekends at your school. Emails, although more impersonal, may be a great way to keep family and friends informed, without the emotion that can seep into phone calls and visits. If you can make it to your fist Thanksgiving break, you are substantially in the clear from homesickness.

Tips: Homesickness is very common. Be aware of how you handle it and make clear choices

Depression

Depression is the most common mental health infliction worldwide. Often depression's onset is late adolescence/early adulthood. Stress is a common trigger for depression and therefore students must monitor their lifestyle decisions in this context.
Depression/stress relievers can take many forms:
Unhealthy- drinking, drugging, hooking-up, vandalism, stealing
Healthy- nutrition, proper sleep amounts, exercise, activity, counseling, physician-prescribed medication

Tips: Be self-aware when making decisions, understand why you are doing all activities. Automatic, unhealthy decisions signal a problem.

Seek help when in need, all colleges offer free, confidential counseling.

Substance Abuse

Consider the consequences before choosing to use substances.

Drug and alcohol dependencies usually start in adolescence or early adulthood. **Those who are strong seek help.** Ask the help of a friend or mentor to support your desire for help and see the counseling center. A family history of substance abuse, if not personal experience with your friends, should be enough to have you seriously consider your choices and altogether may turn you off to using.

Be aware that binge drinking can kill. Underage drinking is not advocated and is to be avoided; however if you insist on breaking the law, set a limit of 1 or 2 and stick to it.

If you choose to up your limit, make the choice when you are clear thinking and out of the party environment. Know that at most parties you will be faced with multiple substances that are mind or even life altering. At the very least, a bad decision can impact your night. At worst, a single, bad decision can ruin yours or someone else's life. Most colleges treat underage drinking as the crime that it is. Parents and lawyers need to be involved. Messy and destructive.

Later in life, alcoholics seeking a spouse, look for spouses who are alcoholics because a non-alcoholic person generally does not seek to marry an alcoholic. This is one example of how decisions made in college can impact you for the rest of your life.

It is a choice, and though not seen as so "cool" on Saturday nights in the dorm, choosing activities that are substance free like playing sports, games and or going to the movies are the wiser ways to be engaged. **Choosing friends that agree is the first and likely most important decision you will need to make in this area**. As in most of life, if you choose the right friends and peers, you are that much more likely to succeed.

Alcohol often creates situations where it kills immediately while other drugs, like marijuana, kill slowly by altering brain chemistry… Avoid them all!

Physical and Emotional Safety

Interpersonal Relationships

Developing friendships is often the most rewarding part of life. But because we cannot know what people are thinking, the process of making friends can be challenging, but ultimately rewarding. Be cognizant of others intentions that may be different to yours. Common sense is important to exercise.

Tips: Guys - The truth is, No, really does mean, No! Ignoring this will land you expelled at best and/or with a criminal conviction making it hard to find meaningful employment for life.

Protect yourself and friends from getting into provocative situations. (75% of date rapes occur when one or both individuals have drunk at least one alcoholic beverage.)

Hooking-up

We do not advocate this but, if you make the decision to do so, choose your partners wisely, ask about their backgrounds, and do not pretend to be ignorant of the consequences of your actions. Treat yourself as if you were your best friend.

Know that in life sometimes you only get one chance!

With new freedoms and opportunities to socialize, it is no wonder that STD's are rampant on college campuses. Know that promiscuity can be an unhealthy way that some people aim to cope with their pangs of anxiety, depression, loneliness, and or general feeling of being out of place. Always, keep in mind that your actions have some obvious and some not so obvious physical and emotional consequences. Diseases can be transmitted through most forms of human physical contact. If sex becomes a commodity, easily had and impersonal, it may be difficult to mean more when you want it to mean more.

Tips: Be careful and deliberate in all that you do. The physical, mental, spiritual and emotional risks are great.

Other Physical Safety Tips

False fire alarms are common on college campuses, but respond to all as if they are real. You may never know if it was a real alarm!

Know the location of all fire alarms, fire extinguishers and exits. Count the number of doors to the exit in case you need to find it in the dark or in smoke.

Use only power strips that are over-current protected.

Do not drape towels on lamps.

Avoid halogen lamps which can reach 900 degrees or greater. Especially avoid top-heavy torch style floor lamps with halogen bulbs. Two fire hazard dangers associated with these lamps include curtains blowing into the lamp and lamps tipping over.

Keep all appliances unplugged when not used.

Do not use multiple extension cords as these cause fires.

Do not overload elevators, this can cause an elevator to stop mid-way, resulting in severed limbs or death.

Seek identification for repair people entering your room or dorm.

Look out for each other. If you see someone suspicious, tell the RA and campus police.

Beware of how you use ATM's. Do not count money there and have papers prepared before you enter a bank ATM.

Beware of people taking your photo and beware of video cameras. You could end up on the web, unwittingly.

Finances
Credit cards are often offered to college students on campus. Be careful. These need to be repaid and your credit score is starting to be calculated already. Credit scores can make the difference in future home mortgage and car loan interest rates. Meaning, if you are foolish with credit, the cost to buy a home or a car is more expensive, maybe prohibitive. Be careful and pay all balances in full each month!

Cults
In addition to credit card companies, cults are happy to sell their wares by recruiting on college campuses because they know college students are starting to figure out their places in the world and can be idealistic. Be wise and be very careful and research thoroughly any organization to which you will associate.

Grades
As you may have learned in high school, it is harder to bring down a great GPA, than to build one from a weak foundation. Work extra hard in your first and second semesters to start with a strong GPA. You will be very happy you did as you progress to the harder junior and senior year courses.

GETTING OUT IN FOUR

Today, more than 62% of college students are taking six years to earn a four year degree. Why? Lack of focus. If you know your major, great, you have some focus. Those who are undecided also have focus when remembering that your job in the first two years is to embrace the core curriculum and take direction from your interests there so that by junior year you are better attuned to the world and your place in it, ready to select a major.

In addition to lost time, taking 6 years to earn the bachelors increases college costs by 50%. How to stay ahead of the credit curve?

Take a full credit load each semester of 15 credits (on a three credit per course system, which is typically five courses per semester). At most colleges, you can be considered a full-time student, with financial aid, at as low as an 11 credit course load. Even consider taking an 18 credit semester (six courses) when the courses may not be as demanding (normally the first two years of college).

Stay ahead of the credit curve by taking summer classes. Most colleges accept transfer credits from other colleges, especially those from the gen ed, distribution requirement or core courses. Normally, you see the department chair at your college with the course description from the local community college, online college or other college. The chair signs a form, you take the course in the summer and it counts toward your degree when you return on the fall with your summer grade transcript.

The GREAT First Year of College

Housing

Substance-free, chemical-free, quiet, study and wellness all are names of these types of dorms on the many campuses. The parties still go on, and you can still go. The parties are just not in your face 24/7, they are not in your room, and no one is vomiting on your bed.

For students, who have had experiences with substance abuse, who prefer quiet areas to study, make the choice to be in the quieter, substance-free dorms. All students would be better served there.

Activities

Find clubs and organizations that don't revolve around a keg.

Service, volunteer, athletic, spiritual or religious organizations are good to seek out because they usually look beyond the upcoming weekend in their activities. Feeding the homeless at night feels much more gratifying the next day than a kegger!

Stay physically active, even if you hop on an elliptical or treadmill for 20 minutes, 5 days a week. That could be the start of a healthy lifelong habit, one of many that college will offer. College students are flocking to the fitness center in higher numbers; you will not be alone there! Enjoy intramurals; they are fun!

Making Positive Connections

Perhaps the single greatest factor that will make or break your college career is whether you connect with an adult who will mentor you through your academic choices and other significant choices at college.

Mentors are important to have and are great to consult with. Seek out a professor you admire and ask his or her permission to be your mentor. All this entails is an occasional meeting to discuss anything from majors and academics to life decisions and friends. Most will say yes. Seek their counsel in both academic and personal challenges.

Be mindful of potential conflicts with opposite-gender mentors.

Administrators, professors and classmates are all people with whom you will develop relationships. You will both contribute to and learn from all of these relationships. Align yourself with the right people and your college experience will be all that you hope it will be and much more!

Preserve your Faith!

Keep your faith alive. Many people lose their faith in college as parents are no longer watching and you are completely independent.

It is just for these reasons that you **do** want to maintain your relationship with God. He will be needed more than ever.

In the first week of school (it gets harder the longer you wait), be sure to connect with a faith-based group, all colleges have them. There too you will find friends who will support and encourage your positive development, as you will support and encourage theirs!

Grow and enjoy the experience!

APPENDIX 1: MAJOR DIFFERENCES BETWEEN HIGH SCHOOL AND COLLEGE

HIGH SCHOOL		COLLEGE
At least 30 hours/week of classroom instruction; regular daily schedule; attendance enforced	**Schedule**	Usually 12 hours/week of classroom instruction; classroom attendance often not checked
Routines established and enforced by parents, school, community traditions	**Freedom**	Student alone responsible for scheduling free time; time management skills needed
Regulations of school and home limit number of distractions	**Distractions**	Frequent distractions (parties, fraternities, sports) leading to neglect of academics
Demanded by parents and teachers	**Discipline**	Solely up to the student
More frequent (5 days/week)	**Teacher-Student Contact**	Less frequent (1 to 3 times/week)
Parents, teachers, counselors often take responsibility and arrange tutors, etc.	**Academic Support**	Requested and arranged by student; student must be own advocate even if college offers academic support

Not as great; lower half of class might not attend competitive college	**Competition**	More difficult since only better students go to college
Student's status in academic and social situations often influenced by family/community factors	**New Status**	Student in new situation; judged solely for himself and by his own behavior
Parental contact constant; personalized counseling by teachers and guidance counselors regularly and easily available	**Counseling**	Parental contact limited and difficult; students must seek out counseling; often difficult to schedule and not personalized
Student told what to do in most situations; follow-up on instructions is usual	**Dependence**	Student is on his/her own; much self-discipline required; often no specific time lines, no follow-up, no warnings
Push to achieve and participate from parents, teachers, counselors longtime friends	**Motivation**	Student is on his/her own; push solely from within
Often bases on parental values; student frequently not given choices	**Value Judgements**	New dilemmas with serious implications/consequences involved; outside guidance often not available unless you seek it.

APPENDIX 2: a questionnaire to give your high school college counselor to help them write your recommendation

Comprehensive, Intentional, Developmental

For my school college counselor: Questionnaire

Date: _____

Student Name: _____

Preferred First Name: _____

Academic interest(s) or major(s) you are considering, if any.

_____

_____

_____

How firm are these? 10%   30%   50%   70% 100%

Do you have any diagnosed learning challenges?

Have you had educational testing for diagnosed learning challenges? If so, when?

1) What are your proudest personal accomplishments? Describe an achievement or experience of which you are especially proud.

2) Describe yourself in five adjectives (I know this is hard, but try, and don't ask your friends).

3) What outside circumstances, if any, have interfered with your academic performance?

4) How many siblings do you have, if any, and what are their ages? Are they currently enrolled in college or graduated? If so, where?

5) Do you have religious beliefs? If so, are you seeking to attend college with like-minded students?

6) Please detail any leadership experience you may have had, in and out of high school.

7) Has any high school years summer experience or study been of significant importance to you? Please explain.

8) What course(s) have you enjoyed most? Why?

9) What course(s) have given you the most difficulty? Why?

10) In what subjects did you work hardest?

11) In what subjects did the grades come easiest?

12) Are your high school grades an accurate measure of your ability and potential? If not, why?

13) Have you had any paid employment (part-time or summer) in your high school career, such as babysitting (include employment the summer before ninth grade and plans for this summer)? If so what did you do, when and approximately how many hours per week were consumed? (List employers, positions, and duration.)

Employer Position   **# of Hours**   **Part-Time School/Summer**

_____

_____

_____

14) Including school requirements, what community service/volunteer work have you performed (including service trips, babysitting, tending to a relative in need, any and all religious activities, etc.) and approximately how many hours per week/# of weeks have you committed to each volunteer activity?

15) What are your hobbies or, what do you do when you are not in school or doing homework? Include: conditioning, playing and practicing an instrument/sport, hanging out with friends, pc, the arts, snowboarding, long boarding, writing and everything else! Approximately how many hours per week do you spend on each activity?

16) Please list your high school activities and any high school awards and distinctions you have earned.

17) What is your most time consuming activity, not counting school work, and how many hours per week do you expend on this activity approximately?

18) Is there any other information you would like to share with me so that I can make an accurate appraisal of colleges and universities that will fit you?

19) How far from home are you willing to attend college, assuming there are no financial issues with that? Is there anywhere you do not want to go? (Minutes away, an hour away, day's drive, plane ride)

20) Have you considered taking a year off before going to college and, if so, what would you like to do in that year?

21) If your parent(s) graduated from college and or graduate school, from which colleges/graduate schools did they graduate?

22) Are there any colleges that you or your family feel strongly about (either pro or con) If yes, which ones and why?

23) When thinking about your college search process, I am most excited about…

24) When thinking about your college search process, I am most worried about…

25) Which talents make you stand out?

26) Do you like reading outside of school? What kinds of things

27) In which areas do you need to strengthen your skills—writing, public speaking, study habits, etc.)?

28) What are your longer term goals—graduate or professional school, other?

29) Have you challenged yourself or taken academic risks in high school? In what ways?

30) Do you work better when you are challenged by tough classes and motivated classmates or when you are near the top of a less competitive group?

31) Write about your learning style: In what ways do you learn best? Identify what kind of teaching style that works best for you.

32) How much academic or personal support will you need in college? (i.e. strong advising system, tutoring, etc.)

33) What are your long-term goals? Graduate school? Law school? Med school? Business? Other?

34) Your intended Undergraduate Academic Interests: Circle those that apply and add any majors that may hold an interest.

Liberal Arts/Humanities	Engineering	Business	Pre-Medicine
Visual Art/Design	Theater/Performing Arts	Communications	Pre-Law
Science/Math	Music	I have no idea	

35) (Circle One) I have already made use of…

Prep Class

Online Prep Class

Prep Tutor

Other Prep:_____

36) If you are interested in college level athletics, indicate the sport and Division.

37) If you feel that your SIGNIFICANT artistic and creative abilities and accomplishments may be a component in the college admissions process, indicate that here.

38) Athletics, Arts, Everything! Be certain to list the level of your participation (JV, Varsity, etc.), and your specific role or leadership position within the activity. If you have won any kind of recognition, list that as well. If you are active in something outside of school, please list this.

	Fall	Winter	Spring
9			
10			
11			

39) **In order of importance,** list just those activities, arts, and/or sports that have meant the most to you and briefly explain why.

40) **Family**

Indicate those schools that have granted degrees to either of your parents/guardians:	Mother	Father
Parent/Guardian Job/Employer		
Indicate those schools that have granted degrees to any other member of your immediate family.	Name and Relationship	School
Indicate the college in which you have a sibling enrolled now or next year.		
Indicate any college in which there is a strong family interest.		
I am a first-generation college bound.		
Circle One YES NO		

41) IF YOU WISH, please indicate any ethnic, racial, religious information and/or , circumstances that you suspect might be of interest to college admissions.

42) **College Qualities** Circle the quality or qualities you wish to be present in your college/university. If uncertain, feel free to circle any that are acceptable to you.

State University	Single Sex	Private University	Large Greek Presence- Fraternities and Sororities	Religious Affiliation
				Urban
				Suburban
Liberal Arts College	Liberal Social and Political Culture	Conservative Social and Political Culture	Research University	Rural

43) How long is your daily commute to high school? Round Trip / One Way?

44) Indicate   a 5 if there is a strong interest in a category

a 3 if interest is somewhat strong

a blank if you are indifferent, or

a 1 if you are opposed to a certain category

Location Feel free to circle those states that are appropriate		Size of School		Type of Institution-applicable ONLY if you have particular undergraduate interests	
Mid-Atlantic-MD, NY, NJ, PA, DE, including DC					
Virginia and the Carolinas		1,000 or less		Technical Institute-Engineering, Design, and Applied Services	
New England-ME, VT, NH, MA, RI, CT					
Mid-West-MO, KN, IA, OH, IL		1,000-3,000		Art Institute-Visual Arts	
Upper MW-MI, WI, MN, SD, ND					
Georgia and Florida		3,000-15,000		Performing Arts-Dance, Theater	
Deep South-TN,MISS, AL, AR, LA		15,000-25,000		Music School/Conservatory	
Rocky Mtn. West-CO, MT, WY, UT					
Southwest-TX, OK, NV, NM, AZ		25,000 +		Military	

APPENDIX 3: college visit organizer

College War Board

College	Address	Counselor Info ses./ tour dates	SAT Mid (+/-/=)	Admit Rate	UG pop/ Grad	in/out state/% white	Intended Major?	Total Cost	Financial points %Need met	Loans/ Grants	Other Coach? Drama/Musi Audition Dates/name

APPENDIX 4: college application organizer

College Application Organizer

		College #1	College #2	College #3	College #4	College #5
College Name						
College Representative						
E-mail						
Address &						
Telephone						
Part 1	Due Date					
(common application)	Done					
	Copied					
	Check/fee waiver	–	–	–	–	–
	Sent					
Teacher						
Recommendations						
Secondary School Report (SSR)						
Midyear Report						
Part 2	Due Date					
	Essay1	–	–	–	–	–
	Essay2					
	Done					
	Checked					
	Copied					
	Postcard					
	Check/fee waiver					
Interview						
	Interviewer					
	Thank You Note					
College testing Requirements		–	–	–	–	–
Extra Materials(tapes,art,add'l recs)						
Application Complete and Sent						
Followup to ensure receipt						

APPENDIX 5 College Athletic Information

For all students remotely considering playing a college level sport, review this essential athletic information (especially if at a division one or two school).

For NCAA Eligibility, there are minimum GPA's and minimum SAT or ACT scores as well. See your college counselor if you are concerned to ensure that you are eligible to compete.

For many students, college athletic participation is an exciting facet of the undergraduate experience. Following are terms with which you should be familiar.

NCAA- National Collegiate Athletic Association

NCAA has three divisions. Generally based on the size of the college and level of competition, Division I include the largest and most competitive colleges and Division III includes the smaller colleges in the NCAA. DII tend to be somewhere in between. It should be noted that many outstanding high school athletes find that Division III still offers a very high level of competition (some high level Division III programs may be more competitive than some Division I or II athletic programs).

To determine a student's projected or potential level of competition students should speak with their coaches.

NCAA Division I

NCAA Division I member institutions have to sponsor at least seven sports for men and women (or six for men and eight for women) with two team sports for each gender. Each playing season has to be represented by each gender as well. There are contests and participant minimums for each sport, as well as scheduling criteria. For sports other than football and basketball, Division I schools must play 100% of the minimum number of contests against Division I opponents - anything over the minimum number of games has to be played with at least 50% other Division I colleges. Men's and women's basketball teams have to play all but two games against Division I teams, and men must play 1/3 of all their contests in the home arena. Schools that have football are classified as Division I-A or I-AA. DIVISIONS I-A football schools usually have fairly elaborate programs. Division I-A teams have to meet minimum attendance requirements. Division I-AA teams do not need to meet minimum attendance requirements. Division I schools must meet minimum financial aid awards for their athletic program, and there are maximum financial aid awards for each sport that a Division I school cannot exceed.

NCAA Division II

Division II institutions have to sponsor at least four sports for men and four for women, with two team sports for each gender. For each playing season (three seasons) they must have both genders competing. There are contests and participant minimums for each sport, as well as scheduling criteria (football and men's and women's basketball teams must play at least 50% of their games against Division II or I-A or I-AA opponents.) For sports other than football and basketball, there are no scheduling requirements. There are no attendance requirements (number of fans per game) for football, or arena game requirements for basketball. There are maximum financial aid awards for each sport that a Division II school must not exceed. DII teams usually feature a number of local or in-state student-athletes. Many Division II student-athletes pay for school through a combination of scholarship money, grants, student loans and employment earning. DII athletic programs are financed in the institution's budget like other academic departments on campus. Traditional rivalries with regional institutions are prevalent on team schedules in many Division II athletic programs.

NCAA Division III

Division III institutions have to sponsor at least five sports for men and five for women, with two team sports for each gender, and each playing season represented by each gender. There are minimum contest and participant minimums for each sport. Division III athletics features student-athletes who receive no financial aid related to their athletic ability, and athletic departments are staffed and funded like any other department in the university. Division III athletic departments place special importance on the impact of athletics on participants rather than on the spectators. The student-athlete's experience is of paramount concern. Division III athletics encourages participation by maximizing the number and variety of athletic opportunities available to students and placing primary emphasis on regional in-season and conference competition.

Student Athlete Registration

By the end of the junior year, Division I and Division II candidates must register with the NCAA Eligibility Center.

See www.eligibilitycenter.org

NATIONAL ATHLETIC INTERCOLLEGIATE ASSOCIATION

The NAIA has 50,000 student-athletes participating at nearly 300 member colleges and universities throughout the United States and Canada. Divided into 14 regions, the NAIA offers 23 championships in 13 sports. Since 1937, the NAIA has continued a long tradition of pushing the envelope and making a positive difference in the lives of students, coaches, and parents. The Champions of Character program is the latest cutting-edge addition to the NAIA's proud history of innovation. Through Champions of Character, the NAIA seeks to create an environment in which each student-athlete, coach, official and spectator, are committed to the true spirit of competition through the five core values: respect, integrity, responsibility, servant leadership and sportsmanship. The NAIA has two divisions in basketball.

Club Sports

Club sports in college are generally well organized can be quite competitive and usually allow students to play other colleges. While it is possible to play more than one varsity sport in college, it is very hard. If you want to play multiple sports then club or intramural (see below) sports may be the way to compete and have fun while limiting heavy commitments and pressure.

Intramural Sports

Intramural sports are the least formal of the three categories of college sports and enable informal teams to play each other, usually within the same college and are often co-ed.

Before the Athletic Visit

Check with high school coaches to help determine your level of competitiveness (DI, DII or DIII) best suited for you.

Check the college website under athletics. There you will find schedules, specific team coach names with email addresses and often a profile form to fill out and submit online. Fill out this profile and email your academic and athletic resumes and letter of interest to the college coach.

Advise the college coach of the expected date of your admissions visit and of the time of your information session and tour (and interview if arranged) and offer to meet him or her when you are on campus. Typically, a coach will email back you and agree to either meet or have an assistant meet with you (if the head coach is not available.) DI and DII colleges may have an assistant coach contact you if it is before July 1 of senior year due to NCAA rules.

From the high school registrar or guidance office, obtain a copy of your transcript, attach it to a resume, make copies and have it ready to give to the coach, even if you have already provided it via email. Be sure to check in with the high school coach often for further advice and follow-up, if necessary.

Check the college website for times, or class (fresh, soph, junior or senior) of athletes in your position. If they are sophs and juniors, coaches are likely recruiting your class for those positions.

When the Athlete Visits

You need to obtain an overall feel for the coaches, their coaching style and the team.

Then you need to discern if those qualities fit your style. Meet with coach, with or without your parents - either is usually fine with the coach. Ask the coach questions that are important to you, such as: academics vs. athletics, proactive substance abuse programs, character of team captains, duration and extent of off-season captains' practices, does the coach want you to apply early etc.? (Make a list of questions, see end of this booklet.) Ask if you are a primary recruit, often indicated if the head coach is speaking directly to you.

Ask which exposure or recruiting camp the coach will be attending this summer and, if you like the coach and the college start to make plans to attend (especially if many of the colleges that you like are all sending their coaches to the same recruiting camp).

Important

For DIII, ask if the coach has influence (pull) in admissions decisions. If the college has early decision, will the coach be able to obtain a "pre-admit" reading of your application (to give you intelligence as to whether or not you will be admitted). This is very helpful information to have, especially if two colleges offer ED. Remember, only one ED application can be submitted and it is therefore important to know if one is a deny from the pre-admit read.

After the Visit

Following a meeting with the coach send the coach a thank you card.

For those colleges you are still interested in attending, have your high school coach contact the college coaches to discuss your skills and your "coach-ability".

Give your high school coach a list of colleges, college coaches, emails and phone numbers when you know the colleges to which you will be applying.

Some myths and realities of college athletics and recruiting

Myth: Enjoying college athletics will not be much different from high school, aside from the skill level.

Reality: Playing college athletics is a significant commitment in time and dedication and will be nowhere close to your high school experiences. In college you play or practice for three seasons: the fall, winter and spring, and you will be required to take lifting and running programs. You may be practicing at 6 AM or midnight, or twice a day, depending upon the facilities available at your school. Summer workout schedules are provided even at the DIII level.

Myth: If I am good enough, coaches will find me eventually.

Reality: Recruiting today is a global process and, despite your skills or successes in high school, it is extremely easy to be overlooked by college coaches who have thousands of athletes to scout and hundreds of potential scouting venues to attend. College coaches do not read your local town paper and neither do they attend your games. Only the top 1% of high school athletes is truly discovered. Students need to assert themselves.

Myth: High school coaches are well qualified to determine if I am college athletic Material.

Reality: While many coaches are qualified, some are not and may never have played their sport in college. Many factors determine whether or not a student can play in college and it is possible that your high school coach may not be the best judge of your potential. Typically though, high school coaches are more invested in your college athletic success than club or AAU coaches.

Myth: All colleges offer athletic scholarships and to all players.

Reality: Only Division I and II colleges can offer athletic scholarships (along with Junior Colleges and NAIA schools). While DI and DII colleges can offer athletic scholarships, after football and basketball, there are many programs that may only have one or two scholarships for their entire team and they may divide that money up among several players. Be sure the college is the right academic fit as well. Also, your scholarship offer is only valid if the head coach makes that offer in writing.

Myth: Division I programs have generous recruiting budgets.

Reality: Some of the larger schools with top notch football and basketball programs do have generous recruiting budgets, but most schools do not. There are very few college coaches that have the ability to fly around the country to recruit players and an endless coaching staff that they can send out to scout, especially if their team doesn't generate money for their school.

Myth: Most athletes receive either a full scholarship or no scholarship.

Reality: Full scholarships are very rare and most coaches divide scholarship money among several top players. The only guaranteed full scholarships are for DI basketball and DI football. Each program is fully funded and offers the maximum number of scholarships allowed by the NCAA: 85 for football, 13 for men's hoops, and 15 for women's hoops. Every other sport and team divides money up among many players, and no other team or program is guaranteed to be fully funded.

Myth: All Division I and II programs offer scholarships.

Reality: While the NCAA mandates how many scholarships a school can offer in a particular sport, it is up to each school to determine whether or not it is willing and able to offer the number of scholarships allotted. Example: Division I baseball programs are allowed to offer 11.7 scholarships to their entire team, but many Division I baseball schools may offer only 3 or 4 scholarships. This will hold true for other sports as well. Check with the coach at the DI and DII colleges being considered, to see what they have historically offered. Students can also ask if they are candidates for those scholarships.

Myth: I shouldn't go to a Division III school if I need scholarship money.

Reality: Many DIII schools offer attractive financial aid programs and you should not overlook a school, even if it does not offer athletic scholarships. Would you rather have $3,000 in scholarship money at a DI school or $20,000 in academic money at a DIII school, and still get the chance to play athletics at the college level? The level of play depends as much on an athlete's passion for the sport as it does ability. Remember grant or scholarship awards can take the place of athletic scholarships.

Myth: Division I programs do not offer walk-on tryouts.

Reality: While walking onto the Kentucky basketball team might be pretty difficult, many coaches rely on walk-ons each year and will usually conduct tryouts to give as many players a chance to tryout as possible. It is better to find out what walk-on opportunities exist before you show up at tryouts. It certainly is not easy, but it is not impossible either. Coaches will be up front about chances so be sure to ask.

Myth: Division III schools are weaker athletically than DI or DII colleges.

Reality: In most cases, yes, but in some cases no. Some Division III schools have very strong athletic programs. They are talented and dedicated athletes who what to continue their athletic careers in college, but want to do so on their own terms. If you think a student can just stroll onto a DIII program you are in for a surprise. Go check out the golf teams at Methodist College (DIII) or the swimming teams at Kenyon College (DIII). In the last 25 years they have about 40 NCAA championships under their belts and they recruit top players from all over the country, many of whom could play some form of Division I athletics had they chosen that route. There are some Division III schools that compete and win against some Division I and II schools. The most competitive DIII conference is the NESCAC (nescac.org), a group of some of the best academic colleges in the world.

Myth: College coaches will help me get into their schools if I excel academically.

Reality: Being recruited by a college coach can give you an advantage over applicants who are not athletes; however you need to be very close academically to what the school is seeking in a student. Sometimes coaches can submit a list of names to admissions, however you need to be committed to the coach and express a strong interest in attending that college. Many students who thought that they were a shoe-in for admission are rejected. DIII coaches can sometimes offer pre-admission reads of your application by admissions, a real plus for ED candidates. See your college counselor for details.

Myth: Good stats or times are enough to earn a scholarship.

Reality: In golf, swimming, and track, tangible scores or times allow you to be measured against other athletes. Stats in team sports are less of a factor because there are so many intangibles such as the class the team competed in, the quality of the competition, etc. Character does, however matter. Coaches and team members want to get to know you as a person and to learn about your work ethic, interests and behavior. Team members will evaluate you when you go to visit. Also, elements completely out of the student's control can determine scholarship awards such as coach's desire to fill a certain position.

Myth: College coaches can contact my family or me anytime they want.

Reality: There are strict rules as to when a coach can send you literature and how often they can contact you at the NCAA level. The rules are less stringent at the Junior College and NAIA level. The good news is that you can contact college coaches any time, so long as you make the phone call. So be sure to speak with, or email, them often.

Myth: If I receive a letter from a coach, I am being technically recruited.

Reality: Coaches send thousands of letters to high school athletes they may or may not have heard of and there are probably 500 kids tearing open the same letter that you received. Receiving a letter means that a coach knows your name and knows that you play the sport they coach. Respond to the letter and follow-up with the coach. Until the coach calls you, invites you to the school and makes you a formal offer to join the program, the letters don't mean too much. In 2004 a DI football program had a list of 4,000 prospects they were sending letters to. Ultimately they were trying to sign 21 players out of a pool of 4,000. Being recruited is rare, which is why the fit of the college in other ways, such as academically, is as important as athletic potential.

8 Facts About College Athletics and Scholarships: What Every High School Athlete Needs to Know- From a Penn State Athletic Director

Over the next few weeks, 400,000 US college athletes will head back to their campuses to begin another year of college sports. But what most parents and high school athletes don't realize is that there is 22 times more academic aid available than athletic scholarships and Olympic sports scholarships usually are in the $3,000-$5,000 per year range. Only two percent of high school athletes receive an athletic scholarship and only 34 percent of college athletes have an athletic scholarship.

During the latest edition of #CollegeChat via Twitter, Weaver (http://twitter.com//collegeathlete) and other college professionals and students discussed facts about college athletics. "I'm afraid that most club coaches are selling parents a bill of goods in chasing after an athletic scholarship," Weaver said. "There can be a lot more availability of academic aid for college athletes at Division III schools which tend to be small private colleges. Aspiring college athletes need to ask themselves what are their priorities?"

Fact 1: Four Year Full Ride Athletic Scholarships are a Myth
Contrary to what parents and high school athletes believe, guaranteed four year full ride scholarships are a myth. The National Collegiate Athletic Association (NCAA) stipulates that athletic scholarships are good for one year at a time and are potentially renewable at the coach's discretion. Coaches that promise full ride 4 year scholarships are not telling the truth. In addition, if an athlete is injured the athlete may lose their scholarship.

Fact 2: Forget Studying Abroad or Participating in Internships in Most DI Programs
In most DI programs it is very unlikely that athletes will be able to participate in studying abroad or working in internships. However, in DII and DIII it is more likely that athletes can participate in studying abroad and internships as well as other campus extracurricular activities.

Fact 3: College Sports May Leave Little Time to Study
Generally, when college athletes are "in season" they may spend 15 to 30 hours per week training and playing in games. In addition, they will also be spending a significant amount of time traveling to games. Therefore, when high school athletes are comparing different colleges, it is extremely important that they find out from other players how much time is required to devote to their sport. Make sure to ask about practice time, weight training time, and travel schedule as well as off-season training.

Fact 4: Hiring an Athletic Recruiter Can Be a Waste of Money

Most college coaches do not like the interference. We recommend that parents and aspiring college athletes do the work themselves High School athletes and parents should also download and read through the NCAA's "2015-2016 Guide for the College Bound Student Athlete" available at http://www.ncaapublications.com/p-4354-2015-2016- ncaa-guide-for-the-college-bound-student-athlete.aspx

We recommend that parents or high school students make the first contact with a coach via email explaining why the student athlete is interested in that college. The email could also include a link to the student athlete's highlight footage on YouTube. Coaches are also interested in a student athlete's scholastic record including GPA, SAT or ACT scores, AP classes and any academic and athletic awards.

Fact 5: College Coaches start building files on 9th graders and on 7th graders for Basketball.
If a budding athlete is interested in playing Division I especially, they or their parents need to make contact with college programs they are interested in as early as 7th grade for basketball or by the end of 9th grade for other sports. We recommend that parents take the helm of the initial phone contact between coach and athlete but need to turn this over to the high school athlete by the time they become a junior. After all, it is very important for the coach to get to know an athlete and the one thing all coaches don't want is a helicopter parent.

Truth 6: You Don't Need to Hire a Professional Videographer to Capture Your Highlights
Save your money and upload your athletic highlights to YouTube recommends Weaver. Coaches don't want to search through DVDs of recruits when they can simply go online and see the latest clips of an athlete on YouTube.

Fact 7: High School Athletes Must take the SAT or ACT and Meet All Academic Eligibility Requirements
The NCAA spells out in detail the academic requirements for DI and DII athletes at http://www.ncaa.org/wps/wcm/connect/public/ncaa/student-athlete+experience/becoming+a+student-athlete/division+i+toolkit
But these guidelines should be used only as a starting point for athletes. Athletes that are interested in competing at more academically rigorous colleges, or at colleges that demand higher academic achievement by athletes for admission, need to make sure they are satisfying the academic requirements of those colleges and not just the NCAA. After all, the NCAA and the coach don't admit an athlete to a college, the Admissions Office does.

Fact 8: College Coaches Send Out Hundreds of Recruiting Letters
Although getting a letter from a college coach can be very exciting and encouraging, aspiring athletes need to keep in mind that coaches send out hundreds of letters like this every year. If a student doesn't have the necessary grades, they will be dropped

from the coach's list. In addition, if your athlete is interested in a particular college that has seen them play either in person or via YouTube, they should ask the coach for an honest assessment of the athlete's chances of making their team.

More Athletic Recruiting Pitfalls

(From www.varsityedge.com)

As a prospective student-athlete, there are many ways to disrupt or ruin the recruiting process and to diminish your chances of having a meaningful college athletic career.

Bad grades and test scores

This is the number eliminator for a student-athlete chances. A student can be the greatest athlete in the world, but if his or her GPA and test scores are too low to get accepted into a college, what difference does it make? A coach really will not care what your athletic skills are until he or she determines whether you can even get into the school. So what is the point of working on your jump shot when you are not even eligible? If you have academic issues, you need to work those out right away or your college career will end after high school. Keep grades high even through senior year.

Bad attitude

This is the second biggest factor that gets many student-athletes in trouble. While coaches like skilled athletes, it is often, **how** you compete and, **how** you interact with your teammates and your opponents that are determining factors in getting recruited. You can attend showcases and camps and show off all you want, but when a coach comes to your game and sees you are not hustling, or that you are yelling at your teammates or complaining to the referees - that can be the end of the process. Coaches don't want players like that and it doesn't take very much for them to stop recruiting you based on one small incident that they witnessed at a game. Keep clean in school and in your community.

Lack of Goals

Some student-athletes are not focused on what they want to do, maybe they want to play college athletics, and maybe they do not. Some want to play two sports or even three sports in college. It is important that you express to college coaches that you are serious about playing the sport you may be recruited for.

Slump in Academics

Many high school seniors think that once they sign on a dotted line or accept a scholarship it is time to party. There have been many revoked scholarships and acceptances to schools because students did no work senior year, got bad grades, and thought that it would not harm them. If you fail English or math in your senior year, you may not be eligible to play college athletics in your college freshman year, even though you graduated from high school.

Legal Problems

Does this need an explanation? One hint of legal problems in your life and coaches from all over the country may stop recruiting you. No matter how good you are, coaches are representing the schools they work for and no one wants an athlete who is going to give that school a negative image. Word travels fast in this day and age.

Injury

Many talented athletes in high school play multiple sports because that is what they have always done. Once you start a sport and are successful at it, it is often hard to stop. If you are serious about your recruiting process you need to consider concentrating on one sport, or two sports that benefit each other. If you are aiming for a basketball scholarship, playing football in the fall of your senior year may not be the best option for you. There are some sports that are mutually beneficial. If you are a football player, running track in the winter or spring is a great way to stay in shape and gain speed and flexibility, and the risk for injury is not as high as other sports. This is a key reason why college/student fit is important beyond athletics, injuries happen.

Poor Performance at a Showcase

Many families are so worried that they have to attend as many showcases as possible that they start to lose focus on each particular one. Quantity is not better than quality and performing well at two showcases will help you more than performing poorly at eight showcases. You also need to evaluate when the showcase takes place and what type of game shape you are in. Many baseball showcases take place indoors in the winter and most players are not in baseball shape. Their running times are slow, their batting is slow, and their fastball is not as fast as it should be. Not only do they end up looking worse, but also they open themselves to the risk of injury because they are trying to get their body to do things they may not have done in a few months. It is important to evaluate each showcase individually and to evaluate how you might perform and how ready you are to perform. Most DI and DII candidates play multiple showcases.

Marketing to College Coaches

Be assertive in letting colleges know who you are and your abilities. Despite the college sports seen on TV, most student athletes are not found.

Make yourself, recognized and ultimately chosen.

Follow the below procedures to improve your chances of playing sports in college.

Important to Consider

Students must be realistic about their athletic talent. College-bound student-athletes must get an honest and accurate evaluation of their abilities from their high school or club team coach.

Can you play Division I, II or is a Division III college more appropriate?

Knowing the answer to this question can save you, and your parents, a lot of work and heartache.

Additionally:

Carefully consider what you are looking for in a college (level of athletic competition, location, size, academic major, etc.)
Be sure to include parents in this discussion!
Speak with your college counselor regarding a balanced approach.

Make contact with the head coaches, or assistant coaches in their absence

Your initial contact might include a

Personalized letter
Athletic resume
School profile (available from school counselor office)
High School team schedule
Follow up with an email to the coach
A request to arrange a meeting when visiting

Other ways to market yourself to college recruiters

Earn the recommendation from you high school coach
Attend summer camps
Play for travel teams
Play in summer leagues
Try out for special tournaments
Promptly reply to a coach's request for information (always be truthful)
Send a video of actual game footage.
Meet players when on campus visiting

Characteristics college coaches look for in recruits

Good Grades

Coaches seek recruits who are motivated both on the playing field and in the classroom. Recruits must meet the academic requirements of a college or university Furthermore, a coach wants to be sure that each recruit will remain academically eligible throughout his or her college career. Coaches desire athletes who can succeed both on and off the playing field.

Leadership

Coaches seek talented athletes and leaders. Leaders are not necessarily the fastest or strongest athletes, but they are important to a team's success. Team captains, for example, are highly regarded for their leadership, dedication and ability to motivate.

Work Ethic/ Dedication

Similarly, coaches desire athletes with a strong, consistent work ethic. A dedicated athlete is not only bound to improve and contribute, he or she will motivate others to train and compete with more intensity. Dedication and hard work are necessary ingredients for success. No discipline issues.

Success

Obviously, coaches pay close attention to an athlete's past results. They are indicative of a recruit's talent and ability to compete and to contribute at the college level.

Potential

Many coaches are more attracted to an athlete's potential than to his or her achievements. In addition to looking at recent stats, coaches may track yearly progress in an attempt to assess an athlete's development and potential. Coaches want to have confidence that in the course of four collegiate years, recruits will improve and remain enthusiastic and dedicated to their sport.

Sample letter of interest- can be emailed

Use this form to open communications with a college athletic program.

April 4, 20xx

John Smith
Head Men's Baseball Coach
University of Texas
Xxx
San Antonio, TX xxx

Dear Coach Smith:

I am John Doe, currently a junior at ---- High School in -City, State--. I am a three-year starting pitcher for the Varsity baseball team and I have been a member of the Miami Premier Club baseball team for six years. I am interested in continuing my athletic career at the collegiate level. In addition to my athletics, I have a strong academic record: a 182 index on the PSAT and a 90% GPA. I plan to take the SAT in January.

I am starting my preliminary college search and I am requesting more information on your athletic program. Miami interests me due to the strong business program and the strong baseball program. I am familiar with Southwest Conference baseball and I feel that my skills would be sufficient to compete at that level.

If you are interested in learning more about me, I would be happy to send you a full resume of my accomplishments, links to a short highlight video, and the names of coaches who have agreed to be references.

Thank you for your time. I look forward to hearing from you.

Sincerely,

Fred Doe

Enclosed: My athletic and academic resumes as well as my game schedule

What this Letter Tells a Prospective College Coach

Your academic qualifications
Your position and a brief description of your success
That you are familiar with the school's academic program and athletic conference. Big plus!
You have a video available

What to Do Next?

In about two weeks, follow up with a phone call to the coach. Coaches are looking for mature, confident athletes, who are interested in their program. "Hi, this is (your name) from (name of school). I sent you a letter a couple of weeks ago and I wanted to call and introduce myself." Then pause and wait for his/her reply.

Before speaking with a coach by phone consider role-playing a potential conversation with a family member or college counselor. The more serious and intentional you sound by phone the more likely a coach will be to keep you in mind.

A Note on Recruiting or Scouting Services

Many prospective student-athletes and parents will be made aware of, or receive mailings from, outside organizations that offer to aid you in garnering attention from college coaches.

Many of these organizations exist, and student-athletes and parents should proceed with caution.

Most college coaches say they prefer the athlete and his or her family to do the "marketing" and that they read student developed materials more carefully than those sent by a company.

Sample Athletic Resume- Use with already prepared academic resume

---

Fred Doe

Your address

Home phone, cell phone, email address,   date

Class of 2019

Athletic Information

     School: North High School

     Sport: Baseball

     Position: Pitcher

     North High School: #1

     Miami Premier Club Baseball Jersey: #2

     40-yard time: 4.5

Personal Information

     Height 6'1"

     Weight 175 lb.

Sports (Baseball) Background

     2017/2018 (Junior Year)

     Team District Champs (North High School)

     Team Regional Finalists (North High School)

     Team 1st Place, Miami Premier Club Baseball

     2016/2017 (Sophomore Year)

     Team District Champs (North High School)

     Team Regional Finalists (North High School)

     Team State Runner-up (North High School)

     Team 2nd Place, Miami Premier Club Baseball

Awards/Honors

Varsity, Team Captain, North High School (2017)

First Team All-District (2017)

Varsity Awards: Best Defensive Player (2016) Coach's Award (2017)

Additional Information

Other Sports: Soccer - Varsity (11-12)

Camps: University of North Carolina Baseball Camp (Summer 2017)

Indiana University Baseball Camp (Summers 2016,2017)

References

Mr. Bob Jones	Mr. Charles Marco
Head Coach Varsity Baseball	Head Coach
North High School	Miami Club Baseball
68 North 152nd Street	2226 SE 14th Avenue
Miami, FL 33359	Miami, FL 33308
(305) 233-2000 ext. 6	(305) 223-5578

Sample General Questions for Athletes

Are tutors available for athletes?

Are workout rooms available with separate equipment?

Are there special dining hall hours to accommodate practices?

Is there access to medical/training support?

Are there any preferential class registrations to accommodate training/game schedules?

Do academics come first?

Can an athlete go home for winter break and other breaks?

Are summers impacted? Can an athlete have a summer job?

What sort of substance abuse education does the athletic department provide, if any?

Can you describe the character/moral strength of the team captains?

How many players do you plan to graduate this year and how many openings do you anticipate?

Do you offer walk-on tryouts?

I see you took a major trip last year, is this something you do every year? (A good question is one where you show knowledge of the program)

Is there a particular system you like to adhere to? (I.e. 3-pointers, frequent substitutions) This is less likely of an issue in sports where a strategy or philosophy is less a factor such as track or cross-country.

How much influence does a coach have in admissions decisions?

Other Athletic Questions

Questions to ask Coaches

Where am I on your priority list?
Where do you project me?
What are my playing opportunities?
How do you handle injuries in the scholarships renewal process?
What physical requirements need to be met over the summer?
What academic support programs are in place?
How do you handle missed practices?
How do you handle missed classes?
Is summer school required?
What is the average SAT/ACT of the team?

Questions for Players

What does your typical daily schedule look like? In season and out of season?
How many hours a night do you study? What is your GPA?
Do you have an academic advisor? Is he or she helpful?
What do you think of the quality of education at this school?
Generally, how do you see student-athletes regarded by the student body?
If you had to do it over, would you still choose this school?
Do the coaches and players seem to care about each other?
Were the coaches and players honest and friendly or did they seem phony?
Were the coaches interested in academics?
Did they ask me about my major and career intentions?
How will I feel if one or more of the coaches I enjoy leaves?
Would I attend this school if I had no intention of competing?

Coaches who offer a position

Am I your number one choice and will you wait for an answer, or have you offered more than one person and plan to take the first one who responds?
How much time do I have to accept your offer? I have some other visits to make and I want to be fair to all.
If you are not interested, write back and say thanks but no thanks.
Finally, all student athletes should ask themselves, will I be happy at the college? If, for any reason, you become injured and are unable to play athletics, will you be happy there?

NOTES

Made in the USA
Middletown, DE
19 July 2022